PACK OF LIES

Hugh Whitemore

# PACK OF LIES

OBERON BOOKS
LONDON

WWW.OBERONBOOKS.COM

This trade edition first published in 2012 by Oberon Books Ltd
521 Caledonian Road, London N7 9RH
Tel: +44 (0) 20 7607 3637 / Fax: +44 (0) 20 7607 3629
e-mail: info@oberonbooks.com
www.oberonbooks.com

A catalogue record for this book is available from the British
Library.

PB ISBN: 978-1-7831-9791-0

Cover design by James Illman

# Characters

BOB

BARBARA

JULIE

HELEN

PETER

STEWART

THELMA

SALLY

*Pack of Lies* by Hugh Whitemore was first presented by Michael Redington in association with Bernard Sandler and Eddie Kulukundis at the Theatre Royal, Brighton, on 11th October, 1983, and subsequently at the Lyric Theatre, London, on 26th October, 1983, with the following cast:

| | |
|---|---|
| BOB JACKSON | Michael Williams |
| BARBARA JACKSON | Judi Dench |
| JULIE JACKSON | Eva Griffith |
| HELEN KROGER | Barbara Leigh-Hunt |
| PETER KROGER | Larry Hoodekoff |
| STEWART | Richard Vernon |
| THELMA | Elizabeth Bell |
| SALLY | Penny Ryder |

*Directed by* Clifford Williams
*Designed by* Ralph Koltai

*Pack of Lies* by Hugh Whitemore was presented at the Menier Chocolate Factory, London from 20th September 2018. with the following cast in order of speaking:

| | |
|---|---|
| BOB JACKSON | Chris Larkin |
| BARBARA JACKSON | Finty Williams |
| JULIE JACKSON | Macy Nyman |
| HELEN KROGER | Tracy-Ann Oberman |
| PETER KROGER | Alasdair Harvey |
| STEWART | Jasper Britton |
| THELMA | Natalie Walter |
| SALLY | Sia Dauda |

| | |
|---|---|
| *Creative Team* | |
| *Direction* | Hannah Chissick |
| *Set & Costume Design* | Paul Farnsworth |
| *Lighting Design* | Paul Anderson |
| *Sound Design* | Jon Everett |

# ACT ONE

*BOB enters and addresses the audience. He is in his 40s. He wears a grey suit.*

BOB: I was out in the garden when I heard the doorbell. It was a Saturday afternoon. I was just pottering about, sweeping up leaves and so on, Barbara and Julie had gone shopping. When I opened the front door I found a man and a woman smiling at me, they were holding a Bible and some religious pamphlets. 'We've come to bring you the key to great happiness,' the man said. 'Thanks very much,' I said, 'but I'm happy enough as it is' – and shut the door quickly before they had a chance to say another word. They walked away slowly, still smiling – I could see them through the window. I suppose they were used to having doors slammed in their faces. Later, when I was back in the garden, I thought to myself, 'Well, it's true – I am happy – it's true.' And for a moment I stood there, grinning from ear to dear, just because I felt happy for no particular reason. *(He grins)* It was marvellous.

*Lights up. Day.*

*A small semi-detached house near London, typical of the thousands of suburban homes that were built between the wars.*

*Stage right is the sitting-room: tiled fireplace, net curtains at the bay window, chintz-covered chairs and sofa, small tables, a sideboard, a radiogram, framed paintings of flowers on the walls. Stage left is the kitchen, with a back door leading to the garden. Upstage is the entrance hall and front door, which has a stained-glass panel. A telephone stands on a table beside the stairs leading to the unseen bedrooms.*

*BOB goes to the kitchen where his wife, BARBARA, is preparing breakfast. He sits at the table, picks up the newspaper, and pours himself some tea.*

BARBARA: What's Julie doing?

BOB: I don't know. Getting dressed.

BARBARA: It's almost eight o'clock.

BOB: Yes I told her.

BARBARA: *(Calling.)* Julie! *(To BOB.)* I do wish we didn't have this awful rush every morning.

BOB: It doesn't matter, I'll give her a lift.

BARBARA: Why can't we have breakfast like civilised human beings for a change?

BOB: Well, never mind.

BARBARA: *(Irritated.)* Never mind...!

*JULIE enters. She is a teenager. She wears school uniform.*

JULIE: Sorry.

BARBARA: About time.

JULIE: Sorry.

BARBARA: Every morning it's the same – why do you do it? Rush, rush, rush.

JULIE: I didn't hear the alarm.

BARBARA: That's because you went to bed so late.

JULIE: It wasn't that late.

BOB: When I was your age I was in bed by half-past nine and no arguing.

JULIE: That's just silly.

BOB: No it's not, you need the rest.

JULIE: What's the point of going to bed if I can't sleep?

BARBARA: If you went to bed earlier you'd go to sleep earlier.

JULIE: No, I wouldn't.

BOB: You might.

JULIE: No, I wouldn't. I don't feel sleepy at night – only in the mornings.

BARBARA: Oh, Julie.

JULIE: It's not my fault –

BOB: Nothing ever is.

JULIE: – it's biological.

BOB: What is?

BARBARA: Shall I make some toast?

BOB: What's biological?

JULIE: Feeling tired. Has the postman been?

BARBARA: Julie...

JULIE: What?

BARBARA: Do you want some toast?

JULIE: No thanks.

BARBARA: You've got to eat something before you go to school.

JULIE: I'll have an apple.

BARBARA: That's not enough.

BOB: What's biological about feeling tired?

JULIE: It all depends when you reach your peak. You're either a day person or a night person. *(Biting into an apple.)* You're day people and I'm not.

BOB: Trust you to be different.

JULIE: It's true. These apples aren't very nice.

BARBARA: Have a glass of milk, then.

JULIE: Isn't there anything else?

BOB: Tea?

JULIE: Not at breakfast time.

BOB: What's wrong with tea?

JULIE: Couldn't we have coffee or fruit juice or something?

BARBARA: Fruit juice...?

JULIE: People don't have tea with breakfast any more. It's like having beetroot with salad.

BOB: What are you talking about?

JULIE: So boring.

BOB: What is?

BARBARA: Have some cornflakes. You like cornflakes.

*The front door bell rings.*

JULIE: I'll go.

*She goes to the front door.*

BOB: What on earth is she talking about?

BARBARA: Tell her to eat something.

BOB: She won't listen to me.

*JULIE opens the front door, HELEN and PETER enter; they are carrying a large object (in fact, an artist's easel) wrapped in a tablecloth.*

*HELEN is a tall, large-boned American in her 40s; she invariably wears slacks and sweaters. PETER, her husband, is about 50, also an American; he too prefers casual clothes.*

HELEN: Hi, sweetheart.

JULIE: Hello, Auntie Helen – Uncle Peter.

BOB: *(To BARBARA.)* God, it's Helen, that's all we need.

BARBARA: Ssshhh.

HELEN: *(To PETER.)* Don't push, for Chrissake!

PETER: Sorry.

*JULIE is staring at the tablecloth-shrouded object.*

JULIE: What's that?

HELEN: Surprise, surprise! *(To PETER.)* Back off! – you're pushing it right into my goddam ribs.

PETER: Sorry.

HELEN: *(To JULIE.)* My husband is physically maladjusted, do you know that?

PETER: Maladjusted...?

HELEN: I don't mean maladjusted. Will you open the door please? He malfunctions. What do you call it? No co-ordination – that's the word: co-ordination.

*BOB pushes back his chair and stands up.*

BOB: What's going on out there?

HELEN: No co-ordination, tell him to lift something – he goes right ahead and pushes it.

PETER: That's just not true.

*BOB goes to the entrance hall. HELEN is heading towards the sitting-room.*

HELEN: Door, please, sweetheart! Quickly! *(JULIE hurries to open the sitting-room door.)* Hi, Bob – where is she? Barbara! *(To PETER.)* Mind that table – Jeesus! *(Entering the sitting-room.)* Over there – put it over there. *(Putting the easel by the fireplace.)* Barbara! Where are you? Bar-bara!

*BARBARA enters from the kitchen.*

BARBARA: I'm here.

*With a flourish, HELEN gestures towards the easel.*

HELEN: *(Singing.)* 'Happy birthday to you,
Happy birthday to you,
Happy birthday, dear Barbara...
Happy birthday – to – you!'

*BARBARA stares in amazement.*

PETER: We couldn't find any paper big enough – hence the tablecloth.

*JULIE and BOB are spluttering with laughter.*

HELEN: Go on – open it up.

BARBARA: *(Trying not to laugh.)* Oh Helen...

HELEN: What's the matter?

BARBARA: It's not my birthday.

HELEN: Whaat?!

*PETER shouts with laughter.*

BARBARA: It's next week. The twenty-ninth.

PETER: What did I say? What did I tell you?

HELEN: Don't give me that, you said no such thing.

PETER: 'When's Barbara's birthday?' you said, and I said the twenty-ninth.

HELEN: You didn't.

PETER: I did.

HELEN: You didn't.

PETER: I did.

HELEN: *(Turning to BARBARA.)* The twenty-ninth...?

BARBARA: That's right.

HELEN: *(To PETER.)* You said the nineteenth.

PETER: I didn't.

HELEN: You did.

PETER: I swear to you I did not.

HELEN: What are you trying to do to me? Jeesus! It's like that goddam film – what's it called? – you know – Ingrid Bergman thinks she's going crazy, but it's her husband all the time – it's Cary Grant or James Mason or someone –

PETER: Charles Boyer.

HELEN: Charles Boyer – he keeps telling her the wrong things so she thinks she's going crazy – is that what you're trying to do? *(To BOB.)* He said the nineteenth, I know he said the nineteenth.

PETER: If I did, I'm sorry, my mistake, okay? *(To BARBARA.)* Come on, you'd better open it up.

BARBARA: Shall I?

HELEN: I'm sure as hell not taking it back home again.

JULIE: Yes, go on.

BARBARA: All right.

*BARBARA removes the tablecloth. PETER steps forward, helping her to erect the easel.*

PETER: Let me do that. It's a bit tricky.

JULIE: Wow!

HELEN: Well – do you like it?

*BARBARA stands speechless for a moment, unable to find the words to express her delight.*

PETER: It's an easel. For your painting.

HELEN: She knows it's an easel, you dumdum. *(To BARBARA.)* Come on – don't keep us in suspense – do you like it or don't you?

BARBARA: I love it. It's wonderful. I don't know what to say.

PETER: Now that you're going to these art classes, we thought you ought to have all the regular...

*He completes the sentence with a gesture towards the easel.*

BARBARA: *(Overlapping.)* Oh, but it's much too – I mean it's just –

HELEN: *(Overlapping.)* Now don't give me any of that English phoney-baloney about 'Oh, you shouldn't have', and all that horse-shit. You're my very good and dear friend,

Barbara, and if I want to buy you a fancy birthday present, no-one's going to stop me, okay? Okay?

BARBARA: *(Smiling)* Okay.

HELEN: And if it ain't your birthday, who cares, – what the hell – we'll call it a thanksgiving present.

JULIE: Thanksgiving for what?

HELEN: Thanksgiving for what...? *(Improvising rapidly.)* Okay, I'll tell you for what. How many people are there living in London? Six million? Eight? Let's say six, okay? – so that means it was something like three-million-to-one that we'd find ourselves living across the street from folk like you – and if that ain't the cause for some kind of thanksgiving, I don't know what is!

*BARBARA laughs and embraces HELEN.*

BARBARA: Oh Helen – dear Helen – you're priceless!

*Lights fade. BARBARA, HELEN, BOB, JULIE and PETER exit.*

*STEWART enters and addresses the audience. He is middle-aged, lower middle-class but authoritative. He wears a raincoat and a dark blue suit. He might be mistaken for an averagely successful provincial solicitor.*

STEWART: Eventually our investigations led us to a street in Ruislip. It was autumn 1960. Ruislip, I should explain, is a suburb of London. It lies to the northwest of the metropolis and is one of the places one drives past on the way to Oxford. That's how I remember it, at any rate: as somewhere glimpsed briefly through car windows, generally at dusk, generally in the rain – neat rows of semi-detached houses, small front gardens, each with its square of lawn and herbaceous border; bay windows; pebbledash; and every so often, where the downstairs curtains have yet to be drawn, the blue-ish flickering light of a television set. And that, since all stories have to begin somewhere, is where this particular story began for me – or rather this particular chapter of this particular story, for the case as a whole had been occupying my attention for several months. *(He turns to go.)* It is, by the way, by and large – true.

*STEWART exits. Lights up. Dusk.*

*BARBARA and HELEN are coming downstairs. HELEN is wearing an almost-completed dress (some of which is only pinned together) and carrying the dress she arrived in.*

HELEN:  Where do you want me to go?

BARBARA:  Sitting-room.

HELEN:  *(Going into the sitting-room.)* Jesus, it's cold in here. You ought to get central heating.

BARBARA:  *(Switching on the electric fire.)* Well one day.

*HELEN drapes her own dress over a chair and positions herself in the centre of the room.*

HELEN:  What do you want me to do?

BARBARA: Just stand still. I want to make sure it fits all right.

HELEN:  God, you're a fast worker.

BARBARA:  I've got to get a move on if it's going to be ready for Christmas. Hold your arm up. Let me look at the sleeve.

HELEN:  Like this?

*HELEN extends her right arm.*

BARBARA:  Yes, that's fine.

*For a moment BARBARA and HELEN stand facing each other with their arms extended, like ballroom dancers. HELEN, realising this similarity, grabs BARBARA around the waist and whirls her across the room.*

HELEN:  Hey, come on – let's dance!

BARBARA:  *(Protesting but laughing.)* Stop it, Helen, stop it!

HELEN:  *(Singing.)* 'Shall we dance, pom pom pom pom – Shall we dance deedle-eedle' – come on!

BARBARA: *(Laughing.)* Oh Helen, you are a fool!

HELEN: Do you ever go dancing? I never go dancing. I used to love dancing when I was a girl.

BARBARA: Where could you go dancing around here?

HELEN: We could organise something. Why not? We could have dances in the afternoon. What are they called? Tea dances. We could have tea dances in Cranley Drive.

BARBARA: Who'd come?

HELEN: Lots of people, I bet.

BARBARA: All the men are at work. Hold still.

*HELEN stands still while BARBARA checks the hem length of the new dress.*

HELEN: Okay, so we could ask some of the boys from the school.

BARBARA: They're a bit young.

HELEN: Who cares? They're a good-looking bunch.

BARBARA: Some of them. All right. You can get dressed now.

*HELEN changes into the dress she arrived in.*

HELEN: That guy Julie likes – he's really good-looking.

BARBARA: Malcolm Granger?

HELEN: Don't you think?

BARBARA: He's completely unreliable. Have you seen the way he races around on that motorbike of his? He'll get himself killed one of these days.

HELEN: If you're worried, tell her.

BARBARA: I can't.

HELEN: Why not?

BARBARA: She thinks I worry about everything

HELEN: She's right, you do.

BARBARA: I try not to.

HELEN: It's your nature, you can't help it – she knows that, I know that, we all know that. *(She squeezes BARBARA's hand comfortingly.)* Now listen, here's what you do: tell her she's too young to go riding about on motorbikes.

BARBARA: I've told her that already.

HELEN: Then she won't. She's a good girl. She'll do what you say. *(BARBARA, unconvinced, says nothing. HELEN grins.)* You know something? – Malcolm Granger has a beautiful body. I saw him at the pool last summer. Beautiful! Maybe I should lure him round to the house when Peter goes to one of his antiquarian book sales. What do you think? Shall I introduce him to the more sophisticated charms of an older woman? *(BARBARA smiles.)* There are you are, you see, you smiled! It can't be all that bad if you can smile about it.

BARBARA: I wish you'd say something to her.

HELEN: Me...? What can I say?

BARBARA: She'd listen to you.

*HELEN is now dressed.*

HELEN: What about Bob? Why doesn't he talk to her?

BARBARA: You know what Bob's like. She can't do a thing wrong as far as he's concerned. *(Beat.)* Please. There's no-one else I can ask. *(HELEN hesitates.)* Please...

*Beat.*

HELEN: Okay.

BARBARA: *(Relieved.)* Would you?

HELEN: If you think it'll do any good.

BARBARA: Well I do, I really do.

HELEN: Okay.

BARBARA: Oh Helen, dear Helen.

HELEN: Okay, okay.

BARBARA: I hate asking.

HELEN: Don't be silly. *(Deliberately changing the mood, she picks up the unfinished dress and gives it to BARBARA.)* It's beautiful, this dress – really beautiful. You're a clever girl, Barbara. You've got golden hands.

BARBARA: What a funny thing to say.

HELEN: Well it's true.

*JULIE opens the front door; she is wearing a blue raincoat over her school uniform; she carries a satchel.*

JULIE: *(Calling.)* Mum!

BARBARA: *(Calling.)* In here, darling.

JULIE: Hello, Mum. Hello, Auntie Helen.

HELEN: Hi Julie.

BARBARA: *(Kissing JULIE.)* How was choir practice?

*JULIE throws her raincoat onto a chair.*

JULIE: Boring. *(To HELEN.)* Every year it's 'The Messiah'. If only we could do something different. It's so boring doing the same old thing year after year.

BARBARA: Everything's boring as far as you're concerned.

*BARBARA has draped the new dress over the back of a chair. JULIE glances at it.*

JULIE: Is that the dress?

HELEN: Yep.

JULIE: Looks smashing.

HELEN: Doesn't it? You've done a marvellous job, sweetheart.

BARBARA: It's an easy pattern.

HELEN: Don't be so modest. Be proud. If I could make a dress like this I'd be really proud of myself.

BARBARA: You could if you tried.

HELEN: Honey, I could not – and well you know it. I've got five thumbs and no finesse.

BARBARA: Oh, Helen...

HELEN: I remember, when I was a kid, one of the farm hands saying to me – I'd just done something stupid or clumsy or both – and he said to me, 'God help the man you marry, Miss Helen,' he said, 'you may be okay with cattle, but you'll be a disaster in the home.'

BARBARA: Oh what nonsense.

HELEN: He was right.

BARBARA: *(To JULIE.)* Don't start making yourself comfortable, Julie – homework first.

JULIE: Can't I even have a cup of tea?

BARBARA: Do you know what the time is? Your father will be home any minute.

HELEN: Come on, Barbara, give the girl a cup of tea.

BARBARA: You spoil her.

*BARBARA goes to the kitchen.*

HELEN: Well, why not? *(To JULIE.)* Hey – I see the folk down the street are having a bonfire party tomorrow. Are you going?

JULIE: *(Dismissively.)* Oh no.

*JULIE gets up, picks up her satchel, coat, scarf and gloves. She goes to the kitchen and puts her things on a chair at the table. HELEN follows and sits at the table.*

HELEN: *(Smiling.)* Too old for fireworks, huh?

JULIE: I've got better things to do.

*BARBARA is switching on the electric kettle.*

BARBARA: Yes, she's got getter things to do – like homework. *(To JULIE.)* Cake or biscuits?

JULIE: *(Irritated.)* Oh, Mum...? Neither, I told you.

BARBARA: *(To HELEN.)* Have you heard about this stupid diet?

JULIE: It's not stupid. Look at Sue Matthews.

BARBARA: She's always been a big girl.

JULIE: Only because she eats so much.

BARBARA: Well, I think it's ridiculous – someone of your age...

*The phone rings.*

JULIE: I'll go – it's probably Maureen.

BARBARA: Hang your coat up! How many more times?

JULIE: Sorry, sorry.

*JULIE picks up her raincoat and goes to the hall.*

BARBARA: If it's that insurance man, tell him to ring back later.

JULIE: Okay.

*JULIE closes the kitchen door. She hangs her raincoat on a peg and answers the phone.*

BARBARA: Would you like a cup of tea?

HELEN: No, thanks, I'd better get back. *(She watches as BARBARA makes tea for JULIE.)* Say, whatever happened to the Pearsons?

BARBARA: The Pearsons...?

HELEN: Brian and Betty, down at number twenty-three.

BARBARA: They're all right, as far as I know.

HELEN: I've been round there half-a-dozen times and there's never anyone at home. I just wondered if they're okay.

*JULIE returns.*

JULIE: Who's that?

HELEN: The Pearsons.

JULIE: They've gone on holiday. *(To BARBARA.)* It's for you.

HELEN: *(To JULIE.)* At this time of the year?

JULIE: Only for a week. They're back tomorrow.

*BARBARA goes to take the phone call.*

BARBARA: *(To JULIE.)* Who is it?

JULIE: A man.

BARBARA: What man?

JULIE: He didn't say.

BARBARA: Oh Julie.

*BARBARA exits, closing the door. She goes to the phone. JULIE pours tea for herself.*

JULIE: Do you want some?

HELEN: No, thanks. *(JULIE sips her tea; HELEN watches her.)* Well now, young lady, and how are you today?

JULIE: Fine.

HELEN: Good.

JULIE: *(Mock American.)* Fine and dandy.

HELEN: Let's hope it stays that way.

JULIE: *(Glancing at HELEN.)* Why shouldn't it?

HELEN: You tell me.

*JULIE frowns.*

JULIE: What's the matter, Auntie Helen?

HELEN: I thought you weren't supposed to go riding about on motorcycles.

JULIE: Oh.

HELEN: Yes – oh.

JULIE: When did you see me?

HELEN: The other afternoon, with young Mr you-know-who.

JULIE: Malcolm.

HELEN: Yes, Malcolm. I thought all that was strictly verboten.

JULIE: He was only bringing me home from school – and he's very careful.

HELEN: Your mother doesn't think so.

JULIE: You know what she's like she worries about everything.

HELEN: Only because she loves you.

JULIE: She treats me like a little girl. She doesn't realise that I'm grown up – well, almost.

*HELEN looks at JULIE and smiles affectionately.*

HELEN: No. No, I don't suppose we ever will. *(She goes to JULIE and kisses her.)* Okay, I won't say a word, it's our secret. Just take care – you hear me? Don't do anything stupid.

JULIE: I won't. Thanks.

*BARBARA returns.*

BARBARA: What about all that homework, Julie?

JULIE: *(To HELEN, smiling.)* See what I mean?

BARBARA: See what?

JULIE: Nothing. *(She picks up her cup of tea and goes to the door.)* Who was that on the phone?

BARBARA: Someone for your father.

*JULIE slings her satchel over her shoulder.*

JULIE: 'Bye, Auntie Helen.

HELEN: 'Bye, darling – work hard.

JULIE: I will.

*JULIE exits and goes upstairs.*

HELEN: She's a good girl.

*BARBARA finds JULIE's gloves on a chair.*

BARBARA: If only she wasn't so untidy.

HELEN: There are worse things in life than being untidy.

BARBARA: You ought to try living with her. It takes at least half an hour to clear up the mess after she's gone to school: books and clothes all over he place – not to mention all the washing and ironing and mending. She doesn't do a thing for herself, it's disgraceful really.

HELEN: Say what you like – she's a good girl and I'm very fond of her.

*BARBARA glances at HELEN surprised by her uncharacteristically serous tone of voice.*

BARBARA: Yes – well, she's very fond of you.

HELEN: I hope so.

BARBARA: You know she is.

HELEN: I guess I do. *(A sigh.)* I'd give a lot to have a daughter like Julie. You don't know how lucky you are.

*BOB opens the front door. He is wearing a raincoat and a dark grey suit.*

BOB: *(Calling.)* Anyone at home?

HELEN: Hey, there's your old man. I must go.

JULIE: *(Off.)* Hello, Daddy!

HELEN: The dress is beautiful. Truly beautiful. Thank you, sweetheart.

BARBARA: Thank you for listening to all my troubles.

HELEN: Any time. I mean it. Any time.

*HELEN goes to the hall. BOB is taking off his raincoat, which he hangs on a peg by the front door. He is not best pleased to see HELEN.*

BOB: Ah – Helen.

HELEN: Don't look so worried, I'm just going. Is it still raining?

BOB: It's raining, it's cold and it's windy.

HELEN: Only one place to be on a night like this: bed – tucked up in bed, all cosy and warm with the wind whistling outside. A little nooky maybe. Poifeck. Poifeck, as my old Aunty Sophie used to say. *(Grinning at BARBARA.)* Maybe I'll call Malcolm Granger. See if he wants a few mind-broadening experiences. *(Calling upstairs.)* 'Bye, Julie!

JULIE: *(Off.)* 'Bye!

HELEN: *(Blowing a kiss to BARBARA.)* 'Bye, honey.

*HELEN exits, closing the front door as she goes. BOB turns, smiling, to BARBARA, who is standing by the kitchen door.*

BOB: What's all that about Malcolm Granger?

BARBARA: Just a silly joke.

*BOB goes to BARBARA and kisses her on her cheek.*

BOB: Everything all right?

BARBARA: Well, I'm not sure.

BOB: What's the matter*? (Instead of replying BARBARA returns to the kitchen; BOB follows)* What's up?

*BARBARA closes the kitchen door; she turns to face BOB; she is clearly anxious about something.*

BARBARA: Bob, listen – somebody's been ringing up for you – I think it's urgent.

BOB: What is? Who?

BARBARA: His name's Stewart.

BOB: Stewart what?

BARBARA: That's his surname – Mr Stewart.

BOB: Who is he?

BARBARA: I don't know.

BOB: Didn't you ask him?

BARBARA: Of course I asked him. He said he wanted to talk to you, I told him you weren't here and could he ring back later, and he said no he'd like to come round and see us.

BOB: What about?

BARBARA: He wouldn't say – he got all cagey and said he couldn't explain on the phone.

BOB: He's probably one of those Jehovah's Witnesses or whatever they're called.

BARBARA: No, he's something to do with the police.

BOB: The police...?

BARBARA: He said if I was worried about him coming round here, I should ring Scotland Yard and speak to a Superintendent Smith. *(BOB stares at her, but says nothing.)* And he said it's confidential; we mustn't tell anyone.

*Momentarily at a loss for words, BOB walks aimlessly across the room.*

BOB: When did he ring?

BARBARA: About five or ten minutes ago.

BOB: Right – *(He goes to the door.)* – right, I'll talk to this man Smith. What's his number?

BARBARA: I wrote it on the pad.

BOB: Right.

*BOB goes to the phone and dials the number. BARBARA remains by the kitchen door, observing.*

BARBARA: Ask him what it's all about.

BOB: Yes, right. *(On phone.)* Hello? Hello, yes – could I speak to Superintendent Smith, please? My name's Jackson. *(Pause.)* Hello? Is that Superintendent Smith? – Yes, good evening – um – a man called Stewart rang my wife just now and, um – Oh, did he? Yes – Yes – Well, yes, of course if it's – Yes – Yes – um, can you tell me what it's all about...? Oh, I see... Right – Yes, I will – Thank you Superintendent. Goodbye.

*BOB hangs up. He turns to face BARBARA.*

BARBARA: Well...?

BOB: Well, it's obviously pretty important.

BARBARA: What did he say?

BOB: That's what he said: He said it's pretty important, and he'd be grateful if we could spare the time to talk to this Mr Stewart. *(A moment of silence. BARBARA looks at BOB as if she had expected him to make more of a stand.)* He was very polite – very – you know, friendly and pleasant. *(No response from BARBARA.)* What else could I say?

BARBARA: What time's he coming?

BOB: Eight o'clock.

BARBARA: I'd better get on with supper, then.

*Lights fade. PETER enters and addresses the audience.*

PETER: I remember how shy they were when we first met. Helen and I went across and introduced ourselves: 'Hi,' we said, 'we're your new neighbours.' Well, Bob and Barbara stared at us as if we'd just stepped out of a flying saucer. They seemed a little reassured when we told them we were Canadians not American, but even so it took quite a time before they could accept us as regular human beings. They asked us to tea a month or so later, and that's when we first met Julie. 'Julie's short for Juliet,' said Barbara, 'Juliet as in Romeo and Juliet.' Then Bob said, 'We saw the old film with Norma Shearer and Leslie Howard just after we got engaged, and we made up our minds there and then: if we ever had a girl she was going to be called Juliet.' 'And so she was,' said Barbara. 'And so she was,' said Bob. I was touched by the way they would finish each other's stories. It wasn't interrupting, it was more of a mutual orchestration of shared memories, a shared enjoyment of their life together. A kind of celebration. I remember saying this to Helen when we got back home. She pooh-poohed it, said I was being sentimental; but pretty soon after she admitted that she too was beginning to feel a certain affection for them – Julie especially.

*PETER exits. Lights up. Evening.*

*BARBARA and BOB are in the sitting-room, waiting anxiously for Stewart to arrive. The curtains are drawn.*

*A moment of silence.*

BARBARA: What's the time?

BOB: Ten to.

*Pause.*

BARBARA: I wish we knew what it was all about.

BOB: Well, I asked, didn't I? Can't do more than that.

*Pause.*

BARBARA: I keep wondering if it's anything to do with Malcolm.

BOB: Why should it be?

BARBARA: He's been in trouble with the police.

BOB: What sort of trouble?

BARBARA: Something to do with his motorbike. Speeding, I think.

BOB: I thought Julie wasn't seeing him any more.

BARBARA: She still likes him.

BOB: What's that supposed to mean?

BARBARA: What?

BOB: Is she still seeing him or isn't she?

BARBARA: Well, I don't know.

BOB: Haven't you asked her?

BARBARA: Of course I've asked her, but supposing she has seen him – and supposing –

*The front doorbell rings. BARBARA and BOB rise to their feet; they stand facing each other.*

BOB: He's here.

BARBARA: He's early.

*BOB turns to the door but hesitates.*

BARBARA: Quickly! – I don't want Julie to answer the door.

*BOB goes into the hall. BARBARA pats the cushions into shape. BOB opens the front door. STEWART enters. He is wearing a trilby hat, a raincoat and a dark blue suit.*

STEWART: Mr Jackson?

BOB: That's right.

STEWART: Good evening, my name's Stewart. I spoke to your wife on the phone.

BOB: Yes, do come in.

STEWART: Thank you.

*STEWART walks into the hall. BOB closes the front door and goes to the sitting-room.*

BOB: This way.

STEWART: Thank you.

*BOB and STEWART enter the sitting-room.*

BOB: This is my wife. Mr Stewart.

STEWART: How do you do, Mrs Jackson?

BARBARA: How do you do?

*They shake hands.*

BOB: Let me take your coat.

STEWART: Thank you. *(He gives his raincoat and trilby hat to BOB.)* Sorry I'm a bit early. I expected heavy traffic but the roads were empty. All these gales, I suppose. People are staying at home.

BOB: Yes. Yes, I suppose they are.

*BOB takes STEWART's raincoat and hat and hangs them in the hall.*

STEWART: Dreadful floods in the south. Did you hear the news?

BARBARA: No, I...

STEWART: Quite dreadful.

*A brief, rather awkward, silence. BOB returns.*

BARBARA: Do sit down, Mr Stewart.

STEWART: Thank you.

*They all sit. Brief pause.*

BOB: Well – what can we do for you?

STEWART: Is your daughter at home?

BARBARA: Yes, she's upstairs – doing her homework.

STEWART: Would it be possible to disturb her for a few minutes?

BOB: Well, I – *(Anxious hesitation.)* – do you have to see her?

STEWART: I rather wanted to see you all, if that's possible.

BOB: She's not in any trouble, is she?

STEWART: Oh no, good Lord, no.

BARBARA: That's a relief. *(She smiles.)* I'll go and get her.

STEWART: Thank you.

*BARBARA exits. Pause.*

BOB: I spoke to Superintendent Smith.

STEWART: Yes, so he said. *(Beat.)* It's a bit melodramatic, I suppose, ringing Scotland Yard and all that, but – well it's a good quick way of telling people we're – you know – trustworthy – unlikely to run off with the family silver. *(He grins. BOB, too tense for light-hearted pleasantries, merely nods. Brief pause.)* I gather you're with AirSpeed Research?

BOB: Yes.

STEWART: That must be jolly interesting.

BOB: Yes, oh yes, I enjoy it.

STEWART: Travel about a bit, do you?

BOB: Well, not much; up and down to Birmingham mostly.

29

STEWART: Ah. One tends to think of people in the aircraft industry flying off all over the world at the drop of a hat.

BOB: Not me, I'm afraid.

STEWART: Hard luck.

*STEWART smiles at BOB. There is another awkward silence before BARBARA returns with JULIE.*

BARBARA: This is our daughter, Julie.

STEWART: How do you do, Miss Jackson?

JULIE: How do you do?

*STEWART and JULIE shake hands.*

BOB: May I offer you a drink, sir? Whisky? Sherry?

STEWART: No, thanks – but please don't let me stop you.

BOB: No, no, I'm not much of a drinker.

STEWART: Neither am I. *(Small smile; small pause.)* Well now. Where to begin? First of all let me apologise for barging in on you like this. It's a bit disconcerting, I know, when a complete stranger rings up out of the blue, and I'm most grateful for your, ah – for you allowing me to come here – most grateful. The trouble it's, it's a bit difficult for me to explain – precisely – what all this is about, what I do, etcetera, because so much of my work concerns confidential matters, and I'm simply not allowed to discuss them in any details.

BOB: Fair enough.

JULIE: Are you a policeman?

STEWART: Not really, no. I started life as a copper and some of my duties do tend to – what shall I say? – do tend to overlap with those of the police force. In actual fact, I'm a civil servant – *(A grin.)* – and that, as we all know, can cover a multitude of sins. *(He laughs, but nobody responds to his joke.)* Well now – the reason why I'm here. We need your help; it's as simple as that. We've become very interested in one particular chap and we're trying to find out what he does, where he goes, and so on. And the only way we can do that is by asking a lot of rather boring questions. In other words, it's just a straightforward, routine enquiry. All right? There's nothing to be nervous about – it's just routine.

BOB: Who is this man?

BARBARA: Does he live round here?

STEWART: He comes here most weekends. We think he has friends in this part of the world.

*The phone rings.*

BOB: Damn – sorry.

STEWART: Not to worry, not to worry.

*BOB goes to answer the phone.*

BOB: *(On phone.)* Hello? – Oh Maureen – hang on a minute – *(To JULIE.)* – it's Maureen.

JULIE: Tell her I'll ring back later.

BOB: *(On phone.)* She says she'll ring back later – What? – Right – Yes, I'll tell her – Yes, all right – 'bye-'bye.

*(BOB hangs up and returns to the sitting-room.)* She's not coming round tomorrow evening.

JULIE: Why not?

BOB: I don't know. Ring her later. *(To STEWART.)* Sorry.

STEWART: Not to worry. Um – where was I?

JULIE: You were saying about this man coming here to see his friends.

STEWART: Ah yes. Now we don't know who they are or where exactly they live; we don't even know why he comes here so regularly. It might just be friendship, of course, but somehow I rather doubt it.

JULIE: Why?

BARBARA: *(A mild reprimand.)* Julie.

STEWART: He's a busy man, Miss Jackson, and if he takes the trouble to come out here every weekend then I'm sure he does so for a very good reason. And that's why we think it's important to find out as much as we can about these weekly jaunts – and about these mysterious friends of his. Now then – I've got a photograph of him somewhere. *(He finds the photograph in his jacket pocket.)* Yes, here we are. I'd like you all to take a look at it, if you will, and to tell me if you think you've seen him before and if so, where. All right?

*(General murmurs of assent.)* Good. *(Giving the photograph to BARBARA.)* Mrs Jackson...?

BARBARA: *(Looking at the photograph.)* No, I've never seen him.

STEWART: Mr Jackson.

BOB: *(Looking at the photograph.)* No.

STEWART: Miss Jackson.

JULIE: *(Looking at the photograph.)* No, sorry.

STEWART: You're all quite sure.

BOB:          }                    { Yes.

BARBARA: } *(Together.)* { Quite sure.

JULIE:        }                    { Yes.

STEWART: Thank you.

*He puts the photograph into his pocket.*

JULIE: What's he done, this man?

STEWART: I'm afraid I can't tell you that, Miss Jackson.

JULIE: How do you know he comes here at weekends? Has somebody actually seen him?

STEWART: Oh yes, we've been keeping any eye on him for some time.

JULIE: Do you mean following him?

*STEWART smiles at her obvious excitement.*

STEWART: Well, yes, I suppose I do. But it's not as easy as it looks on the films, you know, following people – especially in a place like this, with all these little roads and footpaths – it's worse than the Hampton Court maze. That's why I hoped that one of you might have seen him. It would have saved my chaps a lot of time and trouble.

JULIE: Would you like us to keep a look-out for him?

STEWART: Yes, that would be splendid. *(Quickly adding a few words of restraint.)* But do remember – you must remember – this is all very confidential, not a word to anyone.

BOB: Yes, of course.

STEWART: You do understand that, don't you, Miss Jackson? No whispering secrets to your chums at school.

JULIE: Yes, all right, I promise.

STEWART: Good, excellent, thank you.

JULIE: What happens next? How can you find out where he goes?

BARBARA: Ssshhh, Julie.

STEWART: That's a damn good question; I only wish I knew the answer.

BOB: Well, if there's anything we can do...

STEWART: Thank you very much. *(Taking a notepad from his jacket pocket.)* As a matter of fact, there are one or two things I'd like to ask you before I go – just a few details – *(Opening the notepad.)* – you've lived here quite some time, I believe.

BOB: Over twenty years.

STEWART: Really?

BOB: Since March, 1939.

STEWART: Really? – my word. *(Pen at the ready.)* So you'd know most of the people here in Cranley Drive?

BOB: My wife does, certainly.

STEWART: What about the Matthews at number thirty-eight? Do you know them?

BARBARA: Oh yes, they've been here almost as long as we have. Their daughter's the same age as Julie.

STEWART: And they're English, I take it?

BARBARA: Yes – well, British – Mrs Matthews comes from Cardiff.

STEWART: Right. *(Making a note.)* Then there's the Duncans at number forty...

BARBARA: He's retired – they're both in their seventies – they don't go out very much.

STEWART: And across the road at number forty-five – the Krogers.

BARBARA: Helen and Peter. They're our best friends, really. He's a bookseller.

BOB: Book-dealer. Antiquarian books, you know, first editions.

STEWART: Ah yes.

BOB: They're Canadian.

BARBARA: But they're very nice.

BOB: They've been here about five years.

STEWART: Any family?

BARBARA: }    No.

           } *(together)*

BOB:       }    No.

STEWART: *(Making another note.)* And next to them, at number
forty-three... *(Peering at his notes.)* Can't read my own
writing.

BARBARA: John and Sheila Henderson.

STEWART: *(Writing a correction.)* Henderson, yes.

BARBARA: They both go out to work, so I don't see much of
them. They moved in about a year ago.

STEWART: Right, good. *(Closing the notepad.)* That's very useful,
thank you. *(He puts the notepad into his pocket and turns to
BOB.)* Now you said you might be willing to help, Mr
Jackson.

BOB: Yes, of course.

STEWART: Well, what we have to do is this: we have to station
observers in various parts of the district and find out
where this man goes, where he spends his Saturdays and
Sundays. The problem is – how can our people observe
without being observed? In Piccadilly at rush-hour couldn't
be easier – but here, in these quiet little streets, where
everybody knows everybody else, it's really very difficult.
The observer has to be concealed. There's no other way.
*(Beat.)* So that's what we need. A room. Somewhere. That's
how you can help.

*A moment of silence.*

BOB: You mean a room <u>here</u>...?

STEWART: Just a couple of days: tomorrow and Sunday.

*BARBARA and BOB exchange anxious glances.*

BOB: Well, I don't know about that...

BARBARA: You mean – one of your men – here, in our house?

STEWART: It'd be a young lady. More natural, we thought. If
any questions are asked you can say she's a member of
your Art Club. It is an Art Club you belong to, isn't it, Mrs
Jackson?

BARBARA: *(Amazed that he knows this.)* Well, yes.

STEWART: *(Gestures to the paintings on the wall.)* Are these yours?

BARBARA: Yes.

STEWART: Very good. Very good indeed. *(He smiles at BARBARA and then turns to BOB.)* So what do you think? It seems to me that the small window upstairs would probably be the best –

JULIE: *(Excitedly)* That's my room!

STEWART: A good look-out post, eh, Miss Jackson?

JULIE: Oh yes – perfect.

BARBARA: I'm not too keen on having somebody actually inside the house.

JULIE: Why not?

BARBARA: Julie, please.

STEWART: It's your decision. You must decide.

BOB: Couldn't your people watch from a car – a parked car – couldn't they do that?

STEWART: They could, yes – but not here. That's the point – not here. The roads are far too empty. An unfamiliar vehicle parked for any length of time would be painfully conspicuous. Don't you agree? Painfully conspicuous.

BOB: *(Reluctantly.)* Well, yes...

BARBARA: Why don't you try Helen and Peter at number forty-five? They've got a much better view that we have.

STEWART: I'm afraid we can't go from house to house trying to find the best view. Apart from anything else, we have to make sure that the people we go to are people we can trust – and it takes quite a bit of time to do that.

BOB: To do what?

STEWART: To make the necessary enquiries.

BOB: You mean you've had us screened?

STEWART: We checked. *(A small smile.)* Better to be safe that sorry, after all. And since you're working on classified material at AirSpeed Research, we already knew something about you.

BOB: I see. *(Brief pause. BOB is shaken to learn that he has been the subject of a security check; he looks at BARBARA and then back to STEWART.)* So it really is important, then...

STEWART: We think it might be, yes.

BOB: What about... I mean – would it be dangerous?

STEWART: Dangerous...?

BOB: Well, presumably this man's committed a crime of some sort.

STEWART: He's not a thug, if that's what you mean. There's no danger of any physical violence.

BOB: But he is a criminal...?

STEWART: Let's say we have reason to believe that he's involved in some kind of illegal activity.

*BOB turns to BARBARA.*

BOB: What do you think?

BARBARA: It's up to you.

*BOB hesitates for a moment; then he turns to STEWART and nods his approval.*

BOB: All right, then. *(To BARBARA.)* All right?

BARBARA: *(She nods.)* All right.

STEWART: Thank you. Thank you very much indeed.

*(To BARBARA.)* Would half-past nine tomorrow be convenient?

BARBARA: Um – for what?

STEWART: For my girl to arrive.

BARBARA: Oh yes – that'll be fine.

STEWART: Good, splendid. It might be better if she came in through the back garden. It's well hidden from the road and she can use the kitchen door. Would that be all right?

BOB: Yes, of course.

STEWART: Her name's Thelma, by the way. I think you'll like her.

*Lights fade. BARBARA, BOB, STEWART and JULIE exit.*

*THELMA enters and addresses the audience. She in her late 20s, a sturdily built ex-regular army girl. She wears a sweater and slacks.*

THELMA: I noticed that everything had been tidied away. The furniture smelt of lavender polish and there was a vase of fresh flowers on the hall table; it was as if the house had been put on its best behaviour. I went upstairs to the daughter's bedroom. On the chest-of-drawers, a tin of Max Factor talcum powder stood beside a bottle of perfume, shaped like a cat. Holiday postcards from friends were stuck around the mirror. There was a portable gramophone and some records: Roy Orbison and The Everley Brothers. She was reading 'Wuthering Heights'. I could hear the Jacksons moving and talking downstairs. They were talking quietly because there was a stranger in the house. *(Pause.)* The day passed uneventfully and when I left, at half-past five, Mrs Jackson asked me if I had been comfortable. I couldn't help smiling. Surveillance jobs usually mean spending hours, if not days, in cold empty rooms – or, worse crouched in the back of a van. 'Yes, thanks,' I said, 'Very nice,' I said, 'very comfortable.'

*THELMA exits. Lights up. Evening.*

*BARBARA and BOB are seated in armchairs in the sitting-room. BARBARA is sewing and BOB is reading a newspaper. The electric fire casts a cosy glow across the hearth. Pause. BOB yawns and turns a page of his newspaper.*

BARBARA: I wonder where he is.

BOB: *(Without looking up.)* Who?

BARBARA: The man they're looking for. *(No response, brief pause.)* I wonder what he's doing tonight. *(No response; pause; BARBARA raises her head and looks at BOB.)* Perhaps he's married. Do you think he is?

BOB: Stop worrying about it.

BARBARA: I'm not worrying.

BOB: You could've fooled me.

*Pause.*

BARBARA: We don't know anything about him. Nothing. We don't even know what he's done.

BOB: We don't need to.

BARBARA: Because of us he might get arrested. Just think of that. We ought to know something.

*BOB lowers his newspaper.*

BOB: Because of <u>us</u>...?

BARBARA: Because we let them watch.

BOB: *(He grins.)* Trust you to say a thing like that.

BARBARA: Like what?

BOB: Trust you to find a way of blaming yourself. Doesn't matter what it is, does it? – if there's a hole in my sock, if the car breaks down – it's always your fault. Well, this isn't. So stop worrying. *(BARBARA nods her head but her expression remains troubled and anxious.)* Do you fancy a cup of tea?

BARBARA: Do you?

BOB: I don't mind.

BARBARA: A bit later then.

BOB: Right. *(He stands up, stretches, and strolls to the window. He peers through a gap in the drawn curtains.)* It looks as if Helen and Peter are having an early night. Off for a bit of – what

does she call it? – nooky – off for a bit of nooky.
*(BARBARA smiles but remains silent; BOB goes back to his chair.)* I
just can't imagine it, can you?

BARBARA: What?

BOB: All these wild nights we hear so much about. I can't
imagine them actually performing.

BARBARA: Oh, I don't know. Peter's quite attractive.

*BOB glances at BARBARA, mildly surprised.*

BOB: Is he?

BARBARA: Well, not unattractive.

*BOB grins.*

BOB: God, the idea of waking up alongside dizzy Lizzie – the
mind boggles!

*BARBARA smiles. BOB resumes reading his newspaper; BARBARA
sews; a clock strikes the half-hour; BOB turns a page of his newspaper.*

BARBARA: Do you remember that time we saw a man being
arrested outside the tube station?

BOB: When we saw what?

BARBARA: Don't you remember?

BOB: What?

BARBARA: We were going somewhere, the three of us – Julie
was quite small – and we saw these policemen running into
the tube station. Then they grabbed a man and took him
away. Don't you remember? His clothes were all stained
and dirty. I thought he was old at first, an old tramp or
something, but when he walked past I could see he was
young – younger than me. And he was crying. Don't you
remember? I thought it was so sad. He wasn't just crying,
he was sobbing. It was awful.

*BOB stares at BARBARA; there is a moment of silence, before he speaks.*

BOB: What am I supposed to say to that?

BARBARA: I don't know.

BOB: What?

BARBARA: Nothing.

BOB: He might have bashed some old lady over the head and pinched her handbag. Supposing he had. How would you feel about him then?

*BARBARA says nothing; BOB returns to his newspaper. Pause.*

BARBARA: People don't stop being people just because they've done something wrong. They still have feelings.

BOB: *(Firmly.)* Now look – it's nothing to do with us, none of it. Mr Stewart says this man's mixed up with something criminal, something illegal – well, fine, that's all we need to know. Who he is and what he's done just doesn't matter. It's none of our business. *(No response.)* Well, is it?

BARBARA: I don't know.

BOB: Well it isn't. Take it from me. *(He goes back to his newspaper; BARBARA sews; pause.)* Is it the same girl coming back tomorrow?

BARBARA: Yes.

BOB: Thelma.

BARBARA: Yes.

BOB: She seems quite nice.

BARBARA: Yes.

BOB: Must be a bit boring, sitting upstairs all day. Staring out of the window. Not much fun.

*The distant crackle and whoosh of fireworks.*

BARBARA: What's that?

BOB: Fireworks. They're having a Guy Fawkes party down the road.

BARBARA: Oh yes – I forgot.

*Lights fade.*

*BARBARA steps forward to address the audience.*

BARBARA: Sunday. A really beautiful morning, almost
summery, not a cloud in the sky. It must have been about
eleven o'clock when Bob and Julie went out to wash
the car – well, not quite eleven, the church bells were
still ringing. I love the sound of church bells on Sunday
mornings. I'd got a shoulder of lamb for lunch and I'd just
finished doing the vegetables when Thelma came down for
a cup of coffee. We went into the sitting-room and stood
there, by the window. I remember thinking how friendly
she was – not at all what I imagined a police girl would be
like. Then Julie came in for some clean water and told us
about her friend. Maureen Chapman – apparently there'd
been some sort of domestic disaster, she'd let the bath
overflow and the hall ceiling needed redecorating. Julie
asked if she could go around after lunch and help, and of
course I said yes. Well, Thelma and I were both laughing
about that and saying what a mess it must've been, when
Thelma suddenly looked out of the window, I looked out
too, I don't know why, I just did. Helen's front door was
open and somebody was coming out of the house. It was
a man. I'd never seen him before. He didn't look round
to say goodbye. He just hurried to the gate and went off
along the road. He'd disappeared before I realised who
it was. Thelma turned to me and said, 'Did you see what
I saw?' I couldn't speak, I just nodded. It was the man
in the photograph, the man Mr Stewart was looking for.
Thelma went to make a phone call. I just stood there, by
the window. I could hear Julie laughing and talking as
she cleaned the car. The church bells were still ringing.
Although I didn't know what it meant, I felt sure that
something terrible had happened. Then Thelma came
back. 'Mr Stewart's coming to see you this afternoon,' she
said, 'it's very important. Don't tell Julie.' *(Brief pause.)*
Somehow I forced myself to eat some lunch. The meat
kept turning and turning in my mouth. I could hardly
swallow. When Julie went off to paint Maureen's ceiling,

I told Bob what had happened. He gave me a hug. 'Don't worry,' he said, 'there's nothing to worry about.' But as he held me in his arms, I could feel his hands trembling.

*Lights up. Afternoon.*

*BARBARA walks directly into the sitting-room, where BOB and STEWART are waiting.*

STEWART: You actually saw this man yourself, Mrs Jackson?

BARBARA: Yes.

STEWART: You saw him come out of number forty-five Cranley Drive and hurry away along the road?

BARBARA: Yes.

STEWART: And you're quite sure it was the same man – the man whose photograph I showed you?

BARBARA: Yes, oh yes.

STEWART: Yes, I see. *(To BOB.)* Well, it seems you missed all the excitement, Mr. Jackson. You were cleaning the car, I believe?

BOB: Yes.

STEWART: Just here, in front of your house?

BOB: Yes.

STEWART: Yes, well you can see how easy it is for him to come and go without being observed. Amazing, isn't it? *(No response; STEWART strolls across the room.)* He came to Ruislip yesterday lunchtime, that's when his car was seen, anyway. Saturday lunchtime to Sunday morning. Presumably he spent the night with these friends of yours. As per usual. *(STEWART turns to BOB.)* Have you told your daughter about any of this?

BOB: No.

STEWART: Good, that's probably just as well. Don't tell her – for the time being, at any rate. Where is she?

BARBARA: Out with some friends.

STEWART: Good. *(He strolls to the window and looks out.)* Well, what a surprise. It must have been quite a surprise for you, Mrs Jackson; something of a bolt out of the blue, I should imagine. *(No response.)* He was on his way to fetch his car when you saw him. He always parks it outside that block of flats – what's it called? – that block of flats in the next street.

BARBARA: Ruislip Court.

STEWART: Yes, Ruislip Court. He always parks it there. It's an unusual car, you may have seen it, a white Studebaker Farina, licence number ULA 61. Does that ring any bells?

BARBARA: No, sorry.

STEWART: No, well, never mind. *(A small smile.)* Can't imagine why he chose a flashy car like that; singularly inappropriate in his line of business.

BOB: What is that?

STEWART: What?

BOB: What is his line of business? *(STEWART hesitates.)* Can't you tell us what he does, what he's done?

STEWART: Well we're not entirely sure. We think he may have entered the country illegally.

*Pause.*

BARBARA: What does that mean?

STEWART: What?

BARBARA: I don't understand what you mean.

STEWART: We think he may have entered this country with a false passport and under an assumed name: Gordon Lonsdale. *(Brief pause. BARBARA and BOB are both looking at STEWART, clearly waiting for him to say more.)* It's difficult to be absolutely sure. We'll need to make a few more enquiries. It's early days yet.

BARBARA: Yes, but what's he actually done? Why won't you tell us?

*STEWART turns and looks directly at BARBARA.*

STEWART: We think he may be working – covertly – for a foreign government.

BOB: You mean he's a spy...?

STEWART: Something like that – but I'd rather not jump to conclusions until we know a little more.

BOB: *(Almost laughing.)* But what would a spy be doing in Peter's house?

STEWART: Well, quite.

BOB: There must be some mistake.

BARBARA: Shouldn't we tell them? Shouldn't we warn them?

STEWART: All in good time, Mrs Jackson.

BOB: Oh come on – you're not suggesting they're involved with this man, are you?

STEWART: Depends what you mean by involved.

BARBARA: Oh no – not Helen and Peter – they wouldn't do a thing like that.

STEWART: Maybe not.

BARBARA: We've known them for years Mr Stewart – five years!

STEWART: So you said.

BOB: He must be just a casual friend. A business friend.

BARBARA: Another bookseller – something like that.

STEWART: Yes, possibly.

*Silence. BOB goes to the sideboard.*

BOB: I think I'll have a drink. Barbara?
*(She shakes her head.)* Mr Stewart?

STEWART: No, thanks. *(BOB pours a neat scotch for himself. Pause.)* So in all these years, your friends have never spoken about this Mr Lonsdale?

BOB: No, never.

BARBARA: Never.

STEWART: A bit strange, don't you think?

BOB: Why strange?

STEWART: A man who comes to see them most weekends – you'd have thought they'd've mentioned his name at the very least. *(Beat.)* Wouldn't you have thought so, Mrs Jackson?

BARBARA: I don't know...

STEWART: You may be right, of course, he may be just a casual friend, but he's not a bookseller that's for sure. He's a director of a firm called Allo Security Products Limited; they make anti-burglar devices for cars. A bit of a man-about-town; flat near Regent's Park, plenty of girlfriends – not at all the type you'd expect to get pally with the Krogers.

*BARBARA stares at STEWART; vague suspicions are beginning to form in her mind.*

BARBARA: You seem to know an awful lot about him.

STEWART: Not enough, alas.

BARBARA: Are you sure you didn't know where to find him?

STEWART: What do you mean?

BARBARA: Well – I mean – I mean it seems very lucky that you chose our house. Right opposite Helen and Peter's. I mean – it seems almost too good to be true.

STEWART: *(With an easy smile.)* These things do happen, Mrs Jackson.

BARBARA: Do they?

STEWART: We all deserve a little luck from time to time.
*(BARBARA makes no response. STEWART moves smoothly on to the next topic.)* At the risk of sounding a little unfriendly, it's my duty to draw your attention to the Official Secrets Act. We're all bound by it, you know, as we're bound by any other law. I intended to bring the Declarations along for you both to sign – but what with one thing and another, I quite forgot. Not that it matters really. The signing of the Act is just a way, the customary way, of reminding you of its existence and its importance. Legal red tape – and we get plenty of that in my job, I can tell you. All we're asking for is discretion: sensible, reasonable discretion. All right? *(BARBARA and BOB nod their heads.)* Good. Thank you. Well now – tell me about the Krogers.

BOB: Tell you what?

STEWART: Anything. What sort of people are they?

BOB: They're damn good neighbours.

STEWART: Yes, but what do you know about them? Where did they live before they came here?

BOB: Somewhere in south London. Catford, I think.

STEWART: And you said they're Canadians?

BARBARA: Yes.

STEWART: Canadians, not Americans?

BARBARA: Oh no – Helen's most particular about that. I remember once somebody introduced them as an American couple and Helen was really angry; 'Canadian,' she said, 'not American – Canadian!' She almost shouted it.

STEWART: Whereabouts in Canada do they come from, do you know?

BOB: No.

STEWART: No idea at all?

BOB: Helen was brought up in the country somewhere.

BARBARA: She's always telling Julie stories about her life on the farm.

STEWART: What sort of stories?

BOB: How she could climb trees better than any of the boys –

BARBARA: Chop wood –

BOB: Ride horses, all that sort of thing, you know.

STEWART: So she was a real tomboy?

BARBARA: Still is – mind you I'm never quite sure how much of it to believe.

STEWART: Ah...

*The smiles fades from BARBARA's face as she realises the possible significance of her last remark.*

BARBARA: Well, you know – they're just stories she tells Julie. She probably exaggerates a bit.

STEWART: Yes. *(Brief pause.)* What about Peter Kroger? What sort of a person is he?

BOB: Very different from Helen.

BARBARA: Completely different.

BOB: Chalk and cheese.

BARBARA: A marriage of opposites, we always say.

BOB: He's very quiet.

BARBARA: Bookish, you know.

BOB: Intellectual.

BARBARA: Yes, he's an intellectual.

STEWART: And where's his bookshop – in London?

BOB: He used to have a shop in the Strand, but now it's a mail-order business. He sends out lists and works from home.

STEWART: And you'd say they're happy – it's a happy marriage?

BOB: Oh, very.

BARBARA: Very happy, yes.

STEWART: Yes, I see.

*BARBARA bows her head, fighting back tears.*

BARBARA: I do hate talking about them like this.

STEWART: Yes, I'm sorry, it's a most unpleasant situation, I know. Rotten luck.

BOB: So what happens now?

STEWART: Well, obviously it's in everybody's best interest to get to the bottom of, uh – well, whatever's going on –

BARBARA: If anything.

STEWART: If anything. Precisely. We have to find out what this fellow Lonsdale's up to. That's very important.

BOB: Yes.

STEWART: Crucially important.

BOB: Yes.

STEWART: And his relationship with the Krogers: is it just an ordinary friendship, or is – it something more, uh – significant? All of which means, alas, that we'll have to trespass upon your hospitality for just a little longer.

BARBARA: *(Sharply.)* What?

STEWART: The point is this: we think Lonsdale might be in a spot of trouble. He's had a few business problems recently – money problems – and this could make him do something rash – careless. If he does, we need to know about it. And that means keeping an eye on things. And that means keeping somebody here in this house – as from tomorrow, if that's possible.

BARBARA: *(Aghast.)* You mean –

BOB: *(Overlapping.)* Tomorrow? Tomorrow's Monday. You said he only came at weekends.

STEWART: We can't be sure. Things might change.

BARBARA: You mean you want to keep somebody here every day?

STEWART: Just for a week or so.

BARBARA: *(Incredulous.)* Every day...?

STEWART: Well, yes.

BARBARA: Oh, but you can't expect us to do that! It's out of the question.

STEWART: We'd disturb you as little as possible.

BARBARA: No, I'm sorry.

STEWART: And I wouldn't ask if it wasn't really necessary.

BOB: Yes, but look –

BARBARA: What about Julie?

BOB: Yes, what about Julie?

BARBARA: What about her homework?

STEWART: No problem there. It gets dark by – when? four-thirty, five – no point in us staying after that.

BARBARA: Yes, but think how she'll feel; she'll be so upset.

STEWART: Upset...?

BARBARA: Because of Helen and Peter, she's very fond of them.

BOB: She loves them.

BARBARA: She does.

STEWART: Well, there's no reason to worry her with details.

BOB: We'll have to tell her something.

STEWART: Just stick to the original story: just say it's a routine investigation.

BARBARA: She won't believe that.

STEWART: Why not? Children accept things very easily.

BARBARA: She's not a child.

BOB: There must be an easier way of finding out.

STEWART: I only wish there were.

BOB: Why don't you just go across and ask them?

STEWART: You mean the Krogers?

BOB: Yes.

STEWART: Ask them what?

BOB: What they know about this man and what he was doing there this morning.

STEWART: Yes, but suppose they're involved with him in some way?

BARBARA: Oh, but they're not, I know they're not.

STEWART: Suppose they are.

BARBARA: They're not.

STEWART: Just suppose. We can't afford to take the risk. *(Beat.)* Well, can we?

BARBARA: Why bother to ask? You've obviously decided what you're going to do – why bother with us?

STEWART: Try to look at it from my point of view, Mrs Jackson. Lonsdale was seen coming out of their house. You saw him yourself. We can't ignore that. We can't pretend it never happened. We have to act accordingly. We have to.

*Pause.*

BOB: So what are you saying, what are you suggesting?

STEWART: I'm suggesting that this present arrangement should continue – for a week or so. That's all. Nothing more.

BARBARA: I don't think you understand. Helen and Peter are our best friends. We see them every day.

STEWART: Yes, I know.

BARBARA: Helen, specially, she's always popping in.

STEWART: Yes, I know.

BARBARA: Well, you can't expect me to talk to her and drink cups of tea with her when I know there's somebody spying on her in Julie's bedroom. I can't do that, I'm sorry, I can't – I won't.

STEWART: Perhaps you could try – just for a day or two.

BARBARA: Why should I?

*Always the peacemaker, BOB recognises a bellicose tone in BARBARA's voice; he turns pacifically to STEWART.*

BOB: It's asking a hell of a lot, you know.

STEWART: *(Quietly.)* I'm afraid I must insist.

BOB: Insist...?

STEWART: Earnestly implore.

BARBARA: It's just not fair, Mr Stewart.

STEWART: It's not, I agree – but being fair has pretty low priority at the moment. I really am very sorry.

*Pause.*

BOB: Would it be the same girl?

STEWART: Well yes I thought so. There might have to be another one – just to give Thelma a bit of a rest. It's an exhausting business, surveillance. Takes a lot of concentration. We'll have a telephone installed upstairs. A separate line, of course. It shouldn't be too irksome for you.

*BOB takes a deep breath; he turns to BARBARA.*

BOB: What do you think?

BARBARA: *(Terse.)* You know what I think.

*Brief pause.*

BOB: Well, if it's only for a week...

*He nods his head, giving reluctant consent.*

STEWART: Thank you, Mr Jackson. *(To BARBARA.)* I find this part of my job very painful and unpleasant. Unfortunately – it has to be done. I'm sorry.

BARBARA: You're wrong about Helen and Peter. It's nothing do with them.

STEWART: Time alone will tell.

BARBARA: They've been such good friends, such close friends.

STEWART: And you think you'd have guessed?

BARBARA: I'm sure we'd have guessed something – just instinctively.

STEWART: My dear Mrs Jackson, people like Lonsdale and his colleagues spend their lives deceiving people like you. It's their job, their profession, and they do it with the greatest skill and conviction. If they didn't, they'd be finished.

*The front door opens and JULIE enters. She is wearing a raincoat over her paint-splattered sweater and slacks.*

JULIE: *(Calling as she enters.)* Mum!

BOB: In here, Julie.

*JULIE takes off her raincoat as she enters the sitting-room.*

JULIE: Oh hello, Mr Stewart.

BARBARA: *(Before STEWART has a chance to respond.)* You're covered in paint! – covered!

JULIE: I know, I know, I'm going to have a bath.

*(To STEWART.)* I've been painting a ceiling and it kept dripping down. *(Turning to leave.)* Any sign of that man?

STEWART: Well –

BOB: *(Hastily imposing.)* Julie, listen – there's been a change of plan: Thelma's not going after all.

JULIE: Oh good.

STEWART: She'll only be here in the daytime – so perhaps you wouldn't mind if she invaded your bedroom again?

JULIE: No, that's fine.

BOB: And you mustn't tell anyone.

JULIE: I know.

BOB: It's important, Julie – not anyone.

JULIE: I know! *(Smiling at STEWART.)* Don't worry Mr Stewart, I won't breathe a word.

STEWART: *(With a smile.)* No, I'm sure you won't.

*(JULIE goes upstairs. Pause.)* Well, there's nothing more to say, is there? *(To BOB.)* Any problems, just ring Superintendent Smith at Scotland Yard.

BOB: Right.

*STEWART turns to leave; he pauses as he passes BARBARA.*

STEWART: Thank you again, Mrs Jackson. I'll do everything I can to make our presence here as unobtrusive as possible.

*STEWART goes to the hall; BOB follows. BARBARA remains motionless for a moment; she then walks across the room and draws the curtains. She switches on the light. Music can be heard from Julie's room upstairs. BOB and STEWART are shaking hands in the hall. STEWART goes out. BOB closes the front door and returns to the sitting-room. BARBARA turns and glares at him.*

BOB: Don't blame me.

BARBARA: I don't want those people here, I don't want them in the house!

BOB: Be reasonable. There was nothing I could do.

BARBARA: You could've said no.

BOB: Well, hardly...

BARBARA: You're always the same with people like that.

BOB: Like what?

BARBARA: You know what I mean: like a schoolboy in front of the headmaster.

BOB: Look, there's no point in –

BARBARA: I don't want them here, Bob – I do not want anything to do with it! *(She turns from BOB and paces across the room.)* And what about Julie?

BOB: What about her?

BARBARA: What are we going to say to her?

BOB: Well, nothing – I mean –

BARBARA: What?

BOB: Well...

BARBARA: Doesn't it worry you – deceiving her like this?

BOB: We're not deceiving her.

BARBARA: We're not telling her the truth. He just told us, didn't you hear him? 'Don't tell Julie,' he said. Didn't that make you feel sick?

*Pause. BARBARA and BOB stand facing each other.*

BOB: Look – there was nothing we could do.

BARBARA: Of course there was.

BOB: We couldn't say no.

BARBARA: Why not?

BOB: Well suppose he's right ...

BARBARA: About what?

BOB: Helen and Peter.

BARBARA: Oh for heavens sake...!

BOB: They obviously know this man.

BARBARA: He's just a friend. What's wrong with that?

BOB: Why have they never mentioned him?

BARBARA: Why should they?

BOB: And we never see them at the weekend.

BARBARA: Of course we do.

BOB: When?

BARBARA: Dozens of times.

BOB: Not once.

BARBARA: What about that trip to the zoo?

BOB: What trip?

BARBARA: When was it? – two or three months ago.

BOB: That was August Bank holiday Monday. We never see
them at weekends, never.

BARBARA: Of course we do.

BOB: Never.

*A moment of silence. BARBARA is staring at BOB. The phone rings.
BOB goes to the hall and answers the phone.*

BOB: *(On phone.)* Hello? – Oh hello, Maureen, just a minute –
*(Calling upstairs.)* Julie! It's for you!

JULIE: *(Off.)* Who is it?

BOB: Maureen.

JULIE: *(Off.)* I'm in the bath – I'll ring back later.

BOB: *(On phone.)* Did you hear that? She's in the bath, she'll
ring later – Right – Right – Yes, all right, 'bye-'bye. *(BOB
hangs up. He returns to the sitting-room. BARBARA has not
moved. They stand facing each other. Pause.)* Shall I ring up
and say we've changed our minds? I'll ring that man at
Scotland Yard. Would you like me to do that? Shall I?

BARBARA: It's too late.

BOB: Why? Why, what do you mean?

BARBARA: You know what I mean.

*BARBARA walks past him and goes to the kitchen. Lights fade. BOB exits.*

*Lights up. Day. Music from the kitchen radio.*

*BARBARA comes in from the garden, carrying some vegetables. She fills a bowl with water and starts to wash and prepare the vegetables. The front doorbell rings. BARBARA looks up; stands very still. Pause. The doorbell rings again. BARBARA switches off the radio. She goes quietly, almost on tip-toe, to the sitting–room and peeps round the edge of the curtains. She springs back. She stands tense and motionless by the window. The doorbell rings again. Very quickly, BARBARA opens a drawer in the sideboard and takes out her paints and brushes; she then walks to the hall and opens the front door. HELEN enters; she is wearing outdoor clothes and carries a shopping basket. PETER follows behind.*

HELEN: Jesus, you were a long time. We thought you must be out.

BARBARA: No, I...

HELEN: Weren't in the john, were you?

BARBARA: No...

HELEN: *(Walking to the sitting-room.)* If there's one thing I hate it's being hauled out of the john in the middle of it.

*BARBARA closes the front door.*

PETER: How are you, Barbara?

BARBARA: I was just about to do some painting.

PETER: We're not stopping, don't worry, we're just –

HELEN: *(Overlapping.)* We're going up to town, is there anything you want? Hey – how's the easel?

BARBARA: What?

HELEN: The easel – is it okay?

BARBARA: Oh yes. Yes it's fine.

HELEN: If it's not, we'll take it back.

PETER: We'll change it.

BARBARA: No, no, it's perfect, I love it.

HELEN: The guy in the store said he'd change it if you didn't like it.

PETER: *(To HELEN.)* She says it's fine, she loves it, what more can she say? *(Going to the door.)* Come on, let's leave the girl in peace.

HELEN: What's the hurry?

PETER: The whole idea was to get up to town before the crowds, remember?

HELEN: Okay, okay.

PETER: *(To BARBARA.)* We're making an early start on the Christmas shopping. Helen's got a list a mile long. *(To HELEN.)* Show her.

HELEN: What?

PETER: Show her the list.

HELEN: You've got it, I gave it to you.

PETER: You didn't.

HELEN: In the kitchen – you were putting your coat on.

PETER: You put it in your purse.

HELEN: I did what?

PETER: Didn't you?

HELEN: *(Suddenly remembering.)* I left it on the kitchen table – Jesus!

PETER: Are you sure?

HELEN: Sure I'm sure – it's on the goddam table.

PETER: *(Grinning.)* Okay, I'll get it. *(To HELEN, as he goes to the hall.)* I want you outside, in the car, ready to go, in three minutes, okay?

HELEN: Okay.

PETER: *(To BARBARA.)* Take care of yourself.

BARBARA: And you.

*PETER exits. BARBARA, feeling obliged to make some show of using the easel, shifts it forward a little.*

HELEN: Thank God I remembered that list. Just imagine going up to town and forgetting the goddam shopping list! Jeeze! I must be losing my mind. *(She watches BARBARA setting-up the easel.)* So who's the mystery man, huh? And don't pretend you don't know what I'm talking about.

BARBARA: What?

HELEN: Yesterday afternoon – about four o'clock – I saw some guy walking across the street. It looked like he was coming from here.

BARBARA: Well, yes he was.

HELEN: Aha! It's lucky I knew your old man was at home, otherwise I might have gotten very suspicious indeed. Who is he?

BARBARA: Just a friend of Bob's.

HELEN: Yeah, I thought so. Didn't I meet him at your wedding anniversary?

BARBARA: No, that was somebody else.

HELEN: Are you sure?

BARBARA: Quite sure.

HELEN: Gee, that's funny. I could have sworn he was the guy Bob introduced me to. What's his name?

BARBARA: Um. Stewart.

HELEN: Stewart?

BARBARA: He's never been here before, so you can't have met him.

HELEN: Okay, if you say so. *(The easel is now fixed in position; BARBARA starts arranging the tubes of paint.)* Now about this Christmas shopping – what do you think Julie would like?

BARBARA: Oh look, you mustn't bother.

HELEN: What do you mean – bother? It's no bother. I love buying her presents, it gives me pleasure, she's always so appreciative. I was wondering about a blouse, do you think she'd like that? A silk blouse?

BARBARA: Well yes, that would be lovely, but you mustn't be too extravagant.

HELEN: Why not, for heaven's sake? There's nothing I enjoy more than real sinful extravagance. *(She winks playfully.)* Born to be bad, that's me. *(Kissing BARBARA on the cheek.)* I'll see you later, sweetheart. *(Going to the door.)* Do you want anything from the shops?

BARBARA: No, thanks. *(Suddenly, impulsively.)* Oh Helen – we thought we might have some friends round for a drink on Saturday evening. Would you and Peter like to come?

HELEN: We can't this Saturday – what a shame.

BARBARA: What about the following Saturday? We'll change it to Saturday week.

HELEN: I'd better say no. Saturday's always difficult for us. Peter likes to do his accounts at the weekend. But you know that. We told you. *(Going.)* Thanks for asking. Ciao!

*HELEN goes out. BARBARA remains motionless, standing by the easel.*

*Lights fade to black.*

*End of Act One.*

# ACT TWO

*Lights up. Day.*

*The back door opens and THELMA enters from the garden; she is wearing a crash helmet, goggles, a waterproof cape and leggings.*

THELMA: Mrs Jackson? It's me! *(Beat.)* Sally!

> *SALLY walks down the stairs. She is about 30: pleasant, but rather plain: middle-class. She wears a sweater, skirt and raincoat; she is carrying an umbrella. She goes to the kitchen.*

SALLY: You're late.

THELMA: Yes, sorry. There's been an accident on the Western Avenue and the traffic's murder. *(She is taking off her motorbike gear.)* What about that rain – did you see it? I thought the end of the world had come.

SALLY: That motorbike of yours make a hell of a noise; are you sure Mr Stewart said you could bring it?

THELMA: Of course – why not? There are dozens of motorbikes around here. You don't think the Krogers are going to notice one extra, do you? *(Looking around.)* Where's Mrs Jackson?

SALLY: Out shopping.

THELMA: Poor thing, I hope she didn't get caught in that storm. *(She drapes her cape and leggings over a chair.)* God, I'm dying for a cup of tea. How about you?

SALLY: No, thanks.

> *THELMA goes to the sink and fills the electric kettle.*

THELMA: Look, don't worry – I always park it round the corner.

SALLY: *(Puzzled.)* What...?

THELMA: The bike. I park it somewhere different every day – and never outside the house.

*(Switching on the kettle.)* So what's been happening this morning?

SALLY: Nothing much; just routine comings and goings.

THELMA: It's going to be a long job, this one.

SALLY: Do you think so?

THELMA: Don't you?

SALLY: *(A shrug.)* Don't know.

THELMA: Oh yes – this is a biggie. I can smell it. *(Spooning tea into the pot.)* Mr Stewart went to the American Embassy yesterday – twice.

SALLY: How do you know?

THELMA: Sylvia told me. She went out with Bill last night. He was duty driver yesterday, and he told her. Twice in a day! That must mean it's a biggie.

*THELMA takes a bottle of milk from the fridge and puts it on the table.*

SALLY: Don't leave the milk there. You'll have Mrs Jackson tut-tutting at you.

THELMA: *(Not understanding.)* What?

SALLY: She always puts milk in a jug, haven't you noticed? She obviously thinks milk in bottles is common. *(No response from THELMA. She takes a jug from a cupboard and pours the milk into it.)* Can you imagine what her life must be like? Dusting and shopping and ironing and polishing and cooking and washing-up, day after day after day. God, no wonder she's as dull as she is.

THELMA: I like her.

*SALLY looks at her.*

SALLY: Yes, you do, don't you? *(She buttons her raincoat.)* She thinks we're going at the end of the week.

THELMA: Did she say so?

SALLY: Sort of. She keeps dropping hints.

THELMA: Like what?

SALLY: It'll seem strange without you next week, that sort of thing, you know.

THELMA: What did you say?

SALLY: Well, nothing. What could I say? *(THELMA sighs but says nothing; she is standing by the window, waiting for the kettle to boil.)* Right then – I'll be off.

THELMA: Right. *(SALLY goes to the back door.)* Gilbert Harding died.

SALLY: Yes, I heard.

THELMA: Poor old Gilbert. I think it's really sad, don't you? – Clark Gable dying one day, poor old Gilbert the next. *(The front door opens; SALLY and THELMA swing round, suddenly alert. BARBARA enters; she is wearing a raincoat and carrying shopping bags.)* Mrs Jackson?

BARBARA: *(Closing the front door.)* Only me. *(Going to the kitchen.)* What a dreadful morning! – did you see that rain?

SALLY: Wasn't it awful?

THELMA: I thought the end of the world had come.

SALLY: Did you get very wet?

BARBARA: No, I was lucky. *(To THELMA, who is making tea.)* Pour me a cup, would you, Thelma? *(Putting the shopping bags on the table.)* These bags weigh a ton.

THELMA: You ought to get one of those trolley things – shopping basket on wheels.

BARBARA: I know, but they make you look so middle-aged.

SALLY: Is it still raining?

BARBARA: Drizzling – but there's more on the way, by the look of it.

SALLY: I'd better go. *(To THELMA as she goes to the back door.)* I'll see you tomorrow.

THELMA: It's Pat tomorrow – I don't come back till Saturday.

SALLY: Right, I'll see you then. 'Bye Mrs Jackson.

BARBARA: 'Bye Sally.

THELMA: 'Bye.

*SALLY exits.*

BARBARA: She's a nice girl.

THELMA: *(Pouring the tea.)* Milk and two sugars?

BARBARA: Please. *(She starts to unload the shopping.)* I got some sausages for lunch – do you like sausages?

THELMA: I love them, but you really must stop cooking all these meals for us.

BARBARA: I'd hardly call sausages a meal.

THELMA: Mr Stewart would be furious if he knew.

BARBARA: Don't tell him, then.

THELMA: Don't worry, I won't. *(Giving a cup of tea to BARBARA.)* Here...

BARBARA: Thanks.

*BARBARA and THELMA sip their tea.*

THELMA: Gilbert Harding died.

BARBARA: Yes, I heard it on the News. What was it? A heart attack or something?

THELMA: Yes, I think so. Poor old Gilbert. Clark Gable one day, poor old Gilbert the next.

BARBARA: I liked Gilbert.

THELMA: So did I. Grumpy old thing, but I liked him. *(Pause.)* I wasn't too keen on Clark Gable. Not a patch on Gregory Peck. Or Richard Burton. I think he's wonderful. Did you see him on TV the other night?

BARBARA: No.

THELMA: Funny sort of play, but he was wonderful. Those eyes. That voice.

*The front doorbell rings. BARBARA freezes. THELMA gathers together her motorcycling gear and hurries upstairs. The front doorbell rings again. BARBARA goes to the front door and opens it. HELEN enters.*

HELEN: Hi, sweetheart – how are you?

BARBARA: Helen...

HELEN: I've brought this back.

*She displays the cake-tin she is carrying and walks to the kitchen.*

BARBARA: Oh yes, thanks.

*BARBARA closes the front door and follows HELEN.*

HELEN: Those little cookies were deelicious, Barbara. *(She puts the cake-tin on the table.)* So light and crisp – poifeck! How do you do it?

BARBARA: Oh – just a knack.

HELEN: Some knack. *(She turns, smiling, to BARBARA.)* So how's life? Everything okay?

BARBARA: Yes, fine.

HELEN: How's Julie? I haven't seen her for ages.

BARBARA: She's fine – working hard.

HELEN: Come to that, I haven't seen you either. You gave me those cookies on Monday. And here we are – it's Thursday. *(Mock-accusingly.)* Have you been avoiding me, Barbara?

BARBARA: *(Alarmed.)* Have I what?

HELEN: A joke, dear – I was joking.

BARBARA: Sorry, I didn't hear what you said.

HELEN: You're not mad at me, are you?

BARBARA: What?

HELEN: Well, are you?

BARBARA: No, no, of course not. I've been a bit busy, that's all.

HELEN: Busy doing what?

BARBARA: Oh, nothing much.

HELEN: Busy doing nothing much…?

BARBARA: Well, you know how it is.

HELEN: *(Lightly.)* No I don't. I'm beginning to feel like the girl in the bad breath commercial. *(A grin; no response from BARBARA.)* So how's the dress coming along?

BARBARA: The dress…?

HELEN: My party dress.

BARBARA: Almost finished. Ready next week.

HELEN: Terrific. *(She glances at the table and sees two cups.)* Hey, what's all this?

BARBARA: What's all what?

HELEN: Two cups of tea on the kitchen table. Don't tell me you've got a lover hiding away upstairs.

BARBARA: Oh dear – fancy that – I haven't even washed up the breakfast things *(Quickly plunging the cups into the sink.)* – isn't that awful?

*HELEN is staring at BARBARA.*

HELEN: Are you sure you're all right, honey? You look kinda sick.

BARBARA: No, it's nothing, just a headache.

HELEN: Take a pill.

BARBARA: I have.

HELEN: Take another pill.

BARBARA: Yes, all right.

HELEN: I'll go get you one, shall I?

BARBARA: No, please ...

HELEN: You know me: pills and potions keep me going. I'll run upstairs and see what you've got.

BARBARA: No! – Helen! – please! *(Beat.)* Please – please don't fuss!

*HELEN frowns, startled by BARBARA's irritability.*

HELEN: Fuss...?

BARBARA: Sorry, I'm sorry, I didn't mean to be rude.

HELEN: You be just as rude as you like, sweetheart. I mean, Jeeze, if you can't shout at friends, who can you shout at?

BARBARA: I didn't mean to shout, I'm sorry.

*HELEN goes to BARBARA and takes her by the hand.*

HELEN: Look, I tell you what: why don't you put your feet up, go to bed – read a book or something, huh?

BARBARA: Yes, perhaps I will.

HELEN: It'll only make things worse if you try to keep going.

BARBARA: Yes.

HELEN: How about some magazines ... would you like some magazines?

BARBARA: No, please – I don't feel like reading.

HELEN: Are you sure?

BARBARA: I think I'd rather just go to sleep.

HELEN: Okay, you know best. *(She goes to the front door; BARBARA follows.)* Now look – if there's anything I can do, and I mean anything.

BARBARA: Thank you, Helen, you're very kind.

HELEN: Well, for God's sake – what are friends for? *(She smiles at BARBARA.)* Take care of yourself.

BARBARA: You too.

HELEN: Go right upstairs and have a good long rest.

BARBARA: Yes, I will.

HELEN: Good girl. See you tomorrow. Ciao.

*HELEN opens the front door and goes out. BARBARA closes the front door. She shuts her eyes and leans back against the wall. Suddenly she feels the bile rising in her throat; she runs to the kitchen and vomits into the sink. THELMA is walking down the stairs; she pauses half way.*

THELMA: Mrs Jackson...? *(No response.)* Are you all right, Mrs Jackson?

BARBARA: Leave me alone – just leave me alone!

*THELMA hesitates for a moment, and then exits upstairs. BARBARA remains motionless, with her head bowed over the kitchen sink. Lights fade.*

*BOB enters and addresses the audience.*

BOB: As it happened, the war wasn't as bad for us as it was for most people; my job was a reserved occupation, working on aircraft fuel systems, so at least I knew I wouldn't be called up, at least I knew we wouldn't be separated. Even so there was the blitz – not that we had many bombs in Ruislip – hardly any, as a matter of fact but there was always the possibility, always the chance, of something dreadful happening. Every time I heard those damn sirens, my stomach would turn over, God I can feel it now, that terrible lurch in the pit of your stomach – and all the time wondering what I would find when I got home – just bricks and rafters and broken glass, everything gone, Barbara gone, everything just – well, it doesn't bear thinking about. I used to rush back to Cranley Drive just as fast as I could, praying like mad, which was daft because I've never been a believer, never, but I suppose everyone's the same, aren't they, I mean at times like that what else can you do? *(Pause.)* It's always frightened me, the thought of losing her, of being alone, I used to have nightmares about it. But then I'd think – come on, don't be such a chump, there's no point in getting morbid about these things: you're three years older than her and men usually die first anyway, so you'll always have Barbara, there's nothing to worry about, you'll always have her.

*Lights up. Evening.*

*A knock on the back door. BOB goes to the kitchen and opens the back door. STEWART comes in.*

STEWART: Good evening, Mr Jackson.

BOB: *(A hint of surprise.)* Mr Stewart.

STEWART: You are expecting me...?

BOB: Well, yes. Thelma said you might come round.

*They walk to the sitting-room where the curtains have been drawn.*

STEWART: I hope you don't think I've been neglecting you.

BOB: No, no, of course not...

STEWART: I meant to come earlier in the week, but the days just seem to flash by. You know how it is. *(BOB closes the sitting-room door; STEWART turns to face BOB.)* I gather from my girls that your wife is becoming increasingly unhappy with the, um... *(Beat.)* Is she?

BOB: Well, yes.

STEWART: You should have told me. *(Beat.)* There's not much I can do.

BOB: No.

STEWART: You do understand that, don't you? Well, of course you do, I know you do, you're a reasonable man, after all *(Pause.)* What time does she get back from her Art Club?

BOB: Any minute now.

STEWART: Oh good. Would it help, do you think, if I tried to clarify the situation a little?

BOB: How do you mean?

STEWART: Perhaps she feels she's being kept in the dark. Does she? Is that the problem, do you think?

BOB: Well, yes. Something like that.

STEWART: In that case it's a problem easily solved. *(He smiles.)* By the way, I meant to ask – somebody was saying that you and the Krogers have got the same sort of car – is that right?

BOB: Yes.

STEWART: You've both got black Ford Consuls?

BOB: Yes.

STEWART: How extraordinary. *(No response.)* Or perhaps it isn't. What do you think?

BOB: There are plenty of Ford Consuls about – especially around here.

STEWART: True. *(Beat.)* Nevertheless – to find two black Ford Consuls owned by such close neighbours – I must say that strikes me as being rather – well, rather surprising. *(No response.)* How did it happen? Whose car came first?

BOB: Ours. Helen said how nice it was, how much she liked it and so forth – then Peter said they were going to get one exactly the same.

STEWART: Uh-uh. Well, why not? It's a very nice car. *(Beat.)* Is he a car person? Is he interested in cars?

BOB: Not particularly.

STEWART: Just took a fancy to yours...?

BOB: Well, yes.

STEWART: What are his interests? Does he have any hobbies?

BOB: Nothing special. I mean – well, books, of course – apart from that, nothing much.

*(Beat.)* Music, I suppose. He listens to music a lot.

STEWART: On the radio?

BOB: And records. He's got quite a collection.

STEWART: Don't tell me he's one of those hi-fi fanatics.

BOB: Well yes, he is a bit. Stereo sound, FM radio, headphone, all that sort of stuff.

STEWART: Headphones...?

BOB: He likes classical music and she doesn't. Can't stand it. So he listens to his records through the headphones.

STEWART: Well that's one way of avoiding domestic strife, I suppose. What about Mrs Kroger? Does she have a hobby?

BOB: No, not really. She's too much of a Dizzy Lizzie. She tried taking photographs – must've been about a year ago – we did laugh – nothing came out properly – all blurry and out of focus. She spent a fortune on the camera. Poor old Helen.

STEWART: How often do you go to the Krogers' house?

BOB: Hardly ever. Barbara pops in for a cup of tea most weeks, but as far as I'm concerned – it's just, well, four or five times a year – birthdays, Christmas, that sort of thing.

STEWART: Apart from your wife, does Mrs Kroger have any particular friends?

BOB: Depends what you mean by particular friends. She's friendly with everyone. She's a very friendly woman.

STEWART: In what way?

BOB: *(Not understanding the question.)* What?

STEWART: How does this friendliness manifest itself?

BOB: *(Irritated.)* She's just an ordinary friendly woman. She pops in for a chat, she worries if anything's wrong, she takes an interest in people.

STEWART: Takes an interest...?

BOB: *(Fighting back.)* Look, I don't often see her, Mr Stewart. I'm at work when she comes round. Barbara's the one she talks to, not me. I don't know what she does or what she says. Anyway, there's nothing sinister about being friendly, is there?

STEWART: Nothing sinister, no. It just adds to the pattern.

BOB: What pattern?

STEWART: Well if the Krogers are mixed up in this business – and I say if – if they are, then it'd be essential for them to know what's going on in Cranley Drive – any change of routine, any change of neighbour – well, it could be dangerous for them.

BOB: You can make anything look suspicious if you try hard enough.

STEWART: True.

BOB: I mean all that stuff about the cars. Why shouldn't they buy a car like ours if they want to?

STEWART: No reason at all – on the other hand, it could be construed as an extremely clever thing to do.

BOB: Clever? Why?

STEWART: Because it would certainly confuse anyone who might be watching them. I mean, if one of my chaps saw a black Ford Consul parked in Cranley Drive he couldn't be sure, at a glance, whether the Krogers were at home or whether you were. Could be useful, that. *(BOB stares at STEWART but says nothing.)* It's not terribly important, I agree – it's just one of those little details that tend to arouse interest; and it's only when you start adding all these things together that a significant pattern begins to emerge.

*The front door opens and BARBARA enters; she is wearing her tweed coat and carrying a shopping bag filled with oil-paints and brushes.*

BARBARA: *(Calling.)* Hello, it's me.

BOB: *(Calling.)* We're in here.

*BARBARA registers the use of 'we'; she goes to the sitting-room.*

BARBARA: Mr Stewart.

STEWART: Do forgive me for dropping in like this, I just wanted to make sure that everything is all right. *(Beat.)* Is everything all right?

*BARBARA puts down her shopping bag and unbuttons her coat.*

BARBARA: I thought the girls would be leaving last weekend.

STEWART: Well – no, I'm terribly sorry.

BOB: Mr Stewart says he'll explain.

BARBARA: First it was two days, then a week, then two weeks – how much longer?

*STEWART responds with a friendly smile.*

STEWART: Let me put you in the picture, shall I? Let me tell you something about the background to this case. It won't solve your problems, I know, but it may help you live with them for just a little longer.

*Brief silence. BARBARA turns to BOB.*

BARBARA: Have you offered Mr Stewart a cup of tea?

STEWART: Thank you, Mrs Jackson, I never drink tea in the evening, I find it keeps me awake.

*BARBARA goes to the door.*

BARBARA: I'll just take my coat off.

*BARBARA goes to the hall and hangs her coat on a peg. STEWART turns to BOB.*

STEWART: Julie's gone to the cinema, I believe?

BOB: Yes.

STEWART: Yes, I thought it would be a good idea to come when she was out. Fewer complications. *(A smile.)* And the fewer of them the better, eh? *(Pause.)* What has she gone to see?

BOB: Um – I'm not sure. *(To BARBARA, as she returns.)* What's Julie gone to see?

BARBARA: 'The Millionairess'.

STEWART: Oh that's frightfully good. We enjoyed it enormously, Peter Sellers is marvellous, first class.

*BARBARA turns abruptly to STEWART.*

BARBARA: Look since you're here, there's something I must tell you.

STEWART: *(Friendly.)* What's that?

BARBARA: I don't know how much longer I can go on like this.

*Silence. The chill change of atmosphere is almost tangible.*

STEWART: Yes. Yes, I'm sorry.

BARBARA: Apart from anything else, I'm worried about Julie – she's got so much work to do for her O-levels, and all this is very unsettling for her.

STEWART: Yes, of course.

BARBARA: I know it's important, what you're doing here, but we have got our own lives to lead, after all, and I wouldn't mind so much if you had told us the truth in the first place; you must have known it would be more than a couple of days, you should have told us then.

STEWART: It's always difficult to know how long these jobs will take.

BARBARA: And it's getting worse, much worse.

STEWART: Yes, I'm sure.

BARBARA: Seeing Helen and Peter.

STEWART: Yes.

BARBARA: Every time I see her, every time we speak, every time she comes round – it makes me feel quite ill. *(Beat.)* I can't sleep.

STEWART: Well, if it's any comfort to you, we still don't know how they fit into this, uh – into this particular puzzle.

Obviously they must fit in somehow, I mean as friends of Lonsdale's they must have a place somewhere, but how or where or why, we don't yet know. Maybe they met him in Canada – and since he's travelling on a Canadian passport, that's a distinct possibility, but, at the moment, all we can do is speculate; a futile occupation, if ever there was one. *(Beat.)* Sorry I can't be more enlightening – or reassuring.

BOB: What about Lonsdale? Do you know anything more about him?

STEWART: Anything more...?

BOB: You said he might be a spy of some sort. Is he? You weren't quite sure.

STEWART: Ah, yes. *(He glances at BOB, surprised perhaps, to realise how little information has been imparted.)* Well – well – basically it's all about submarines. Since the last war, submarines have become an increasingly important element in defence – both for us and NATO and – most especially – for the Soviet Union. Russia has a vast fleet of submarines: at least seven hundred, probably more. But the effective value of this fleet has been drastically reduced by the various techniques of underwater detection that have been developed by our NATO boffins – ASDICs, sonar buoys, and so on. Needless to say, Moscow is most anxious to learn the secrets of these devices so that they can be out-manoeuvred and thus rendered useless. And so, spies were sent here to find out all they could. The man in charge of this operation is the man who visits your friends every weekend, the man calling himself Gordon Lonsdale.

BOB: Good God.

STEWART: He's an important chap, make no mistake about that – almost certainly a high-ranking officer in the KGB, Russian Intelligence. And so far, he's been remarkably successful. But the trouble with spying is that you can't always rely on fellow professionals: you often need the help of amateurs. Traitors. And such creatures are notoriously unreliable. Lonsdale needed inside help, and eventually he found a suitable collaborator, an Englishman called Harry. We became interested in Harry about a year ago. He's a naval man and he works at the Underwater Weapons Establishment in Portland. Fiftyish, not much of a career, divorced. Bit of a boozer. He's been boozing more and more just recently – spending a lot of money in local pubs, far more than he can reasonably afford. So where's all that money coming from? We decided to keep an eye on him, and we discovered that he's got a girlfriend – well, woman friend – and she's obviously more than just a friend. What's more, she also works at Portland – in the records section where all the secret material on underwater weapons is filed. They're always together – every evening: drinking, eating in plush restaurants, even coming up to London for occasional weekends. And there's never any shortage of money: cash is clearly no problem. *(Beat.)* They come to London about once a month. They meet Lonsdale. They sell secrets to the Russians. Or so we believe.

*Silence.*

BARBARA: But – but if you think that – why haven't you arrested them?

STEWART: Yes, that's what the Admiralty wants to know. We've had some very sharp memos about it. But the point is, there are bound to be others involved – not just Harry and his girl-friend – not just Lonsdale – there are bound to be several others, and we want to catch the whole lot. That's why we've got to keep watching Lonsdale for just a few more days. The kettle's already bubbling; we must wait for it to boil.

*Silence.*

BARBARA: Do you mean watching Lonsdale or do you mean watching Helen and Peter?

STEWART: I mean watching everyone who's been in regular contact with him. Anyone. And everyone.

*Silence.*

BOB: What about – I mean – are we in any danger?

STEWART: None whatsoever.

BOB: Yes, but what about Barbara and Julie? They're on their own here most of the time and I keep thinking if this man Lonsdale gets frightened or suspicious – what then?

STEWART: There'll be no violence, I can assure you of that. The Soviets don't employ hooligans for this sort of operation.

BARBARA: How can you be sure?

STEWART: Because I am.

BARBARA: How can you be?

STEWART: Because it's my job to be – and I'm very good at my job.

BOB: It's all very well for you, you're used to this sort of thing. I mean all this talk of spies and secret weapons...

STEWART: Yes, it must seem very alarming. I'm sorry.

BOB: Well, it is alarming.

STEWART: Not really, not especially, not as far as you and your family are concerned.

BARBARA: I wish I could believe that.

STEWART: There's absolutely no need to worry, Mrs Jackson; I know what I'm talking about, I have spent most of my adult life studying the supposedly secret workings of Russian intelligence. It's a fascinating task – rather like bird-watching, and as a bird-watcher gets to know the most intimate habits of this favourite species, so I know how these fellows operate, I know their methods. And it's not just guesswork, you'd be amazed what you can find out when you try hard enough. For example, I know more about the KGB Chairman than I do about my next door neighbour. His names's Shelepin – the KGB chap, not my next door neighbour – Aleksandr Nicolaevich Shelepin. He's got a flat in the Kutuzovsky Prospekt – very nice

too, palatial by Soviet standards; and it's furnished with
all those little luxuries that only the chosen members of
the Party elite are able to enjoy: TV, radiogram, piano,
bottles of real scotch in the sideboard. He always has an
early breakfast: eggs, ham, black Russian bread, tea, a nip
of brandy; and then at eight- fifteen, a chauffeur-driven
car takes him to Moscow Centre, the KGB headquarters
in Dzerzhinsky Square. It's quite a pleasant building:
grey stone, looks more Flemish than Russian; it used to
belong to an insurance company before the Revolution.
A harmless-looking place. You wouldn't give it a second
glance. But there's a courtyard tucked away behind, and in
the courtyard is the Lubyanka Prison. Hundreds of people
have died there. Thousands. *(Silence.)* Shelepin's office is
on the third floor. It's got a high ceiling, polished parquet,
a couple of old-fashioned sofas and wood-panelled walls.
There are six telephones on his desk, one of which is a
direct line to the Kremlin. Shelepin works long hours
and there's a bedroom next door in case he's kept late
by some particularly intransigent problem. Sometime,
perhaps, he strolls across the Persian carpet and looks
down at the people hurrying along the Marx Prospekt. He
controls those people and he knows it. They know it too.
You could, I suppose, say much the same about any senior
civil servant looking down at the rush-hour crowds in
Whitehall, but there's one big difference: Shelepin's control
is absolute. *(Silence.)* He's youngish, too: not yet forty-three.
He likes sport – especially football – and he enjoys going
to the theatre. He's also got a weakness for ice-cream,
which is not surprising because Russian ice-cream is the
best in the world. 'Moroshennoe pazhahlsta' is a phrase
that every tourist should memorize; it means 'ice-cream
please.' Anyone who goes to Russia should make a point
of trying the ice-cream. *(A smile.)* And all I know about my
next door neighbour is that his name is Warrender and
that he subscribes to the National Geographic Magazine.
And so the answer to your question is 'no', there is no
danger, absolutely not. The merest hint of any strong-

arm behaviour would cause the most almighty diplomatic rumpus – and that's the one thing the Soviets want to avoid at all costs. So there's nothing to worry about. I guarantee it. All right? Does that put your mind at rest, Mrs Jackson? There's absolutely nothing to worry about.

*BOB and STEWART look at BARBARA, waiting for her response.*

BARBARA: So the girls will be here for some time, then?

STEWART: Well, I hope not – for all our sakes. A few days, perhaps, that's the plan.

BARBARA: Yes, I see. *(She stands up.)* Well, if you'll excuse me, I've got some jobs to do. *(She goes to the door.)* Is that all right? Do you mind if I go?

STEWART: No, no, of course not. Thank you for being so patient.

BARBARA: I don't have much choice, do I?

*BARBARA goes to the kitchen where she starts to tidy away the supper dishes. STEWART turns to BOB and smiles.*

STEWART: I'm not quite sure what I expected her to say, but I certainly expected more than that.

BOB: She never says much when she's upset.

STEWART: No, well – some people don't. *(Beat.)* It must be a frightful strain for her. Appalling.

BOB: Yes.

STEWART: If you think it's getting too much do please let me know. Just telephone Superintendent Smith; I'll pop round any time. *(BOB nods.)* Right. Good. Well – I'd better be going. *(He picks up his scarf and overcoat, which are draped over a chair.)* Don't forget – day or night – don't hesitate to ring. *(Putting on his scarf and overcoat.)* On the other hand, of course, women can be remarkably tough. I've noticed it time and time again. Tough and resilient. More so than many man. Oh yes. *(BOB nods but says nothing. STEWART smiles at him and goes to the kitchen.)* Good night, Mrs Jackson.

BARBARA: Good night.

STEWART: How are my young ladies behaving themselves? No problems in that department, I hope?

BARBARA: Oh no, they're very quiet, very considerate.

STEWART: Good, I'm glad to hear it. *(He turns to BOB and shakes him by the hand.)* I'm most grateful, Mr Jackson. Thank you for being so cooperative. Good night.

BOB: Good night, Mr. Stewart.

*BOB opens the back door. STEWART exits. BOB closes the door. He looks at BARBARA. Aware of his gaze, she glances at him.*

BARBARA: Tea or cocoa? *(No response.)* Tea or cocoa, what do you want?

BOB: Look, I know how you feel, but it was good of him to come here – to tell us those things. He didn't have to.

*BARBARA busies herself at the sink.*

BARBARA: I've decided what to do: I'm not going to think about it. We've got to lead a normal life – for Julie's sake, if not for our own. Let them do what they want. I'm not going to think about it. *(She fills the electric kettle with water.)* Tea or cocoa?

BOB: Tea, I think.

BARBARA: Right. *(BOB makes a move towards her, but she bustles away from him.)* Go and sit down. I'll bring it in.

*BOB hesitates briefly and then goes to the sitting-room.*

*Lights fade. BARBARA addresses the audience.*

BARBARA: Bob's mother was such a frail little thing. I never knew his father, he died long before we met. He was a clerk with an insurance company. She lived alone, Bob's mother, she lived in a small, draughty house in Maidstone. She came to see us twice a year, but always left after a

week – 'I don't want to be any trouble,' she'd say. It was
the most important thing in her whole life: not being
any trouble. When her roof leaked, she refused to tell
the landlord. 'He's been very good to me,' she said, 'and
I don't want to make a fuss.' Even when she was ill and
dying, she wouldn't ring the doctor after six o'clock in the
evening. She'd just lie in bed, all alone in that miserable
house, more worried about making a fuss than anything
else. Her life was governed by fear, bless her heart. She
was afraid of annoying the doctor, afraid of irritating the
landlord, she was afraid of post office clerks, bus inspectors
and anyone in uniform. And, like a child, she thought if
she kept very still and didn't make a fuss, nobody would
notice her. And she was right – they didn't.

*Lights up. Late afternoon.*

*BARBARA goes to the sitting–room. The curtains are drawn. She
fetches a cardboard box, some tissue paper and the now-completed
dress for HELEN. She starts to fold the dress. THELMA walks down
the stairs; she is wearing a raincoat and headscarf. She knocks on
the sitting-room door.*

BARBARA: Come in.

*THELMA enters.*

THELMA: I'm off now, Mrs Jackson.

BARBARA: Don't tell me it's half-past.

THELMA: Mr Stewart said I could leave early.

*Glancing up, BARBARA sees that THELMA is not wearing her usual
motorbike gear.*

BARBARA: No bike today?

THELMA: Trouble with the clutch. *(Seeing the dress.)* What a
lovely dress. Did you make it?

BARBARA: Well, yes.

THELMA: You are clever. It's lovely. Who's it for?

BARBARA: Well, actually – Helen. I promised it to her ages ago.

THELMA: She's very lucky. So are you – having a talent like that.

BARBARA: I wouldn't call it much of a talent.

THELMA: Well, I think it is. I was hopeless at needlework at school. Hopeless at needlework, hopeless at art. Everything I did looked the same: trees, people, buildings – you couldn't tell one from the other. Cats, flowers, elephants – they all looked the same. *(She buttons her raincoat.)* I wish there was something I could do really well.

BARBARA: Oh, I'm sure there is.

THELMA: *(Cheerfully.)* No, there's not, never has been. I can do lots of things sort of half well – but nothing really tip-top. I don't stick at things long enough, that's my trouble. It's what Dad calls my grasshopper mind. *(She grins.)* Well – see you tomorrow.

BARBARA: Usual time?

THELMA: Usual time. I'm coming in instead of Pat. She's got a filthy cold.

BARBARA: Right. *(THELMA goes to the door; BARBARA plucks up courage to summon her back.)* Oh, Thelma... *(THELMA pauses by the door.)* Is there any news?

THELMA: News...?

BARBARA: Yes, news. Nobody tells us anything.

THELMA: Well, no, not as far as I know.

BARBARA: Mr Stewart came to see us.

THELMA: Yes. Yes, I know that.

BARBARA: He told us about that man and his Girl-friend. Harry. And the Russians. He told us what they're doing, what they're trying to find out.

THELMA: Yes.

BARBARA: Did you know he was coming?

THELMA: Well, yes.

BARBARA: You didn't say anything about it. *(No response.)* I suppose he told you not to. *(No response.)* Did he? *(No response.)* He didn't even mention Helen and Peter, I mean he didn't tell us whether they're – you know – actually... *(The sentence drifts way into silence; THELMA says nothing.)* Well, of course they're involved. I mean they must be, it's obvious, any fool can see that. Why didn't he tell us?

THELMA: Well, I can't...

*Pause.*

BARBARA: What?

THELMA: You know I can't tell you anything.

BARBARA: Why not?

THELMA: You know I can't.

BARBARA: *(Angry.)* So you think it's all right, do you, just to let things go on like this?

THELMA: Well, no, I mean –

BARBARA: *(Overlapping.)* You think it's all right, do you? Is that what you think?

THELMA: *(Firmly.)* If I could do anything I would, but I can't.

*Silence. BARBARA sits. Remains motionless.*

BARBARA: To tell you the truth, I don't really care, I don't care what they've done. Helen and Peter. It doesn't make any difference. Not now. Isn't that strange? I really don't care. I cared at the beginning of course. When I first thought, when I first realised – all the deceit and lies and – I was so angry, so hurt – I was so hurt Thelma – and I wanted – well, I don't know what I wanted. I wanted them to be punished, I suppose; I wanted them to be taken away and punished. But those feelings don't last very long, do they? And I keep thinking how kind she's been – and she has been very kind. She's been very kind to Julie. *(Pause.)* I don't care what she's done, she's still my friend. *(Pause.)* I'll tell you what chokes me, Thelma: it's that Mr Stewart not saying anything, not telling us about Helen and Peter, treating us like a couple of kids who can't be trusted. How dare he! *(Pause.)* Can you imagine what it's been like? Can you? *(Pause.)* Last Friday, when I went out shopping, I looked at all the women all around me, and I thought to myself: I'm not like them, I'm not like the others – I may look like them, but I'm not. *(Pause.)* It hurts, telling all these lies, it really hurts. It's like a dead weight on my stomach. It's like grief. You can't forget it. *(Pause.)* And he won't tell us. Why not? Doesn't he trust us? Does he think we're too stupid to understand? Or perhaps he thinks it doesn't matter. *(A shaft of bitterness.)* Well, that's it, of course – why should he bother about us? We're the sort of people who stand in queues and don't answer back – why should he bother about us? He thinks we'll just do as we're told and not ask any questions. *(Pause; then with sudden passion.)* Well, I hate him! I hate him! I want to slap his smug smiling face and say 'How dare you! – how dare you treat us like this! – who the hell do you think you are!' *(Pause; her passion subsides.)* I won't though, will I? Of course I won't. I can say all these things to you because you're just Thelma who likes Richard Burton and sausages for lunch. But I won't say anything to him, and he knows I won't. *(Pause.)* That's how he gets his own way. That's how it works.

*Pause.*

THELMA: Look, I'm sorry.

BARBARA: I bet he knew when he first came here, didn't he?

THELMA: Knew what?

BARBARA: About Helen and Peter.

THELMA: I don't know.

BARBARA: I thought it seemed incredible at the time, seeing Lonsdale that first Sunday.

THELMA: It could have been a coincidence.

BARBARA: Could it?

THELMA: Well, I don't know. Mr Stewart doesn't tell me anything, either. I just do what I'm told.

BARBARA: And I suppose he'd say the same thing, wouldn't he?

THELMA: He might.

*Pause.*

BARBARA: If only it hadn't been Helen and Peter. I lie awake at nights thinking: why them – why? *(Pause.)* This time last year everything was so perfect.

*Pause.*

THELMA: I'll tell you what I think: it's a waste of time looking for reasons. That's what I think. Good things happen, bad things happen. One day you win the pools, the next you fall downstairs. Nobody's to blame. It's nobody's fault. Things just happen. Start looking for reasons and you'll go barmy. Honest. Trust me. Thelma knows. *(They share smiles.)* Can I get you something? How about a nice cup of tea?

BARBARA: You're as bad as my husband. He seems to think a cup of tea'll cure anything. *(She rises to her feet.)* Off you go. The buses'll be packed if you don't hurry.

THELMA: Are you sure you're all right? *(BARBARA nods.)* I'll see you tomorrow. *(BARBARA nods.)* I'm sorry.

BARBARA: It's not your fault.

THELMA: It's nobody's fault. You just remember that.

*THELMA goes to the sitting-room door. The front door opens and JULIE enters, returning from school.*

JULIE: Hello, Thelma, how are you?

THELMA: Fine, thanks – how are you?

JULIE: Fine – where's Mum?

*BARBARA emerges from the sitting-room.*

BARBARA: Here I am. *(She kisses JULIE.)* Had a good day?

JULIE: Pretty gruesome.

*THELMA goes towards the kitchen.*

THELMA: 'Bye then, see you tomorrow.

BARBARA: 'Bye Thelma. I hope you get your bike back soon.

THELMA: Yes, so do I. *(To JULIE, as she opens the kitchen door.)* I'll have to ask your boyfriend to give me a lift. That's a smashing bike he's got. What is it, a Triumph?

*JULIE's mouth falls open in dismay. BARBARA stares at her, appalled.*

BARBARA: Julie...!

JULIE: He was only giving me a ride home.

BARBARA: How many times have we told you?

JULIE: Yes, I know –

BARBARA: *(Overlapping.)* How many times?

JULIE: *(Overlapping.)* Yes, I'm sorry –

BARBARA: *(Overlapping.)* And you promised; you gave me your word!

JULIE: I'm sorry, Mum, I'm sorry!

BARBARA: So that's the sort of daughter I've got – somebody who goes behind my back –

JULIE: *(Overlapping.)* I'm sorry!

BARBARA: *(Overlapping.)* – somebody who lies and cheats!

JULIE: I'm sorry, I'm sorry!

BARBARA: I'll never be able to trust you ever again – never again – never!

*JULIE bursts into tears and runs upstairs.*

JULIE: I'm sorry, I'm sorry, I'm sorry, I'm sorry!

*JULIE exits. A door slams. BARBARA stands trembling and breathless, exhausted by her outburst. Lights fade.*

*THELMA exits. PETER enters and addresses the audience.*

PETER: In the winter of 1932, when the Depression was at its worse, a friend took me to a meeting – an informal and private meeting – in New York City. On our way there we walked along Riverside Drive. Scores of unemployed men were camping there in tiny shacks and shanties. I saw in their faces a degree of hopelessness and despair I had never seen before – and I remembered those brave words about 'life, liberty and the pursuit of happiness.' And I felt a great surge of anger that such noble ideals should have been so betrayed – forgotten. When did it happen – how? When I got to the meeting I found a small group of maybe seven or eight men and women, mostly young, mostly about my age, all talking politics. It was cold that night, and there was no heat in the apartment; we stood around wearing overcoats. An older man read to us from the words of Marx and Lenin. He said 'The ruin of capitalism is imminent. Every attempt to establish a truly human society upon the old capitalist foundations is foredoomed to absolute failure. We are thus confronted by two alternatives, and two only. There must be either complete disintegration, further brutalisation and disorder, absolute chaos, or else Communism.' *(Beat.)* That evening my whole life changed.

*Lights up. PETER goes to the sitting-room and joins BARBARA, BOB, JULIE and HELEN who are grouped around a Christmas tree singing a carol.*

'Joyful, all ye nations, rise,
Join the triumph of the skies;
With the Angelic host proclaim,
'Christ is born in Bethlehem.'
Hark! The herald-angels sing

Glory to the new-born King!'

*JULIE and HELEN cheer.*

HELEN: Hey – wasn't that something?

JULIE: Wonderful!

HELEN: Terrific! Come on, let's have a drink – *(Taking a bottle of sherry from the coffee table.)* – one more little drink…

PETER: *(Stepping forward anxiously.)* I think it's time to go home.

HELEN: Time to go home? Whadya mean – time to go home? What are you talking about? I don't want to go home – I'm having fun!

*(To JULIE.)* How about a drink for you, honey-chile?

*JULIE glances at BOB, seeking his permission.*

BOB: There's some lemonade in the kitchen.

HELEN: Come on, Bob, a glass of sherry won't do her any harm. Let the girl live a little. Jeeze – when I was her age I was drinking bourbon like it was mother's milk!

*She laughs raucously.*

PETER: Helen, please…

HELEN: Get off my back will you? Stop nagging! Don't be such a goddam spoil-sport.

PETER: *(Sharply.)* Helen.

*HELEN swings round to face him: her initial reaction seems to be one of anger; but her mood changes and she becomes immediately contrite.*

HELEN: Okay, okay. Sorry. Loud mouth Helen does it again. 'You never know when to stop – you always go too far' – Jesus, how many times have I heard that! *(Smiling at PETER.)* Okay – just one more little drink, then home. Okay?

PETER: It's getting late.

HELEN: So what? It's Christmas time – I'm with my friends – and I'm happy. Come on; relax. *(To JULIE.)* Hey – do you know what this reminds me of? Christmas at Aunt Sophie's. We always went to Aunt Sophie's when I was a kid – every Christmas. She had the most beautiful little house. Beautiful. And she loved brass – there was brass everywhere: kettles, spark guard, candlesticks, a great brass pot filled with indoor plants. A log fire and gleaming brass. And she'd do everything as it was in the old days as it used to be when she was a child. We always had roast goose and chocolate honey-cake. And there she'd sit, after dinner, my old Aunt Sophie, licking her fingertips to pick up the crumbs of the chocolate honey-cake – and all of a sudden she'd burst out crying. 'What's the matter?' we'd say, 'Why are you crying, Aunt Sophie?' And she'd dry her eyes and blow her nose and lick her chocolaty fingers. 'Nothing's the matter,' she'd say, 'I'm crying because everything's just poifeck.' *(She smiles.)* Well, I guess that's how I feel right now.

BARBARA: Oh, Helen...

*Moved by the story, JULIE goes to HELEN and embraces her. HELEN kisses JULIE on the forehead. The phone rings.*

JULIE: That'll be Maureen.

*JULIE goes to the hall. HELEN looks at BARBARA, BOB and PETER: three unsmiling faces.*

HELEN: Come on, you guys! It's party-time, remember? Jeeze, I've had more laughs at a funeral.

JULIE: *(Calling from the hall.)* It's for you, Dad, Mr Stewart!

*BOB glances sharply at BARBARA. He hurries to the phone.*

*JULIE returns to the sitting-room. BARBARA sits frozen with anxiety.*

HELEN: Stewart – Stewart – where have I heard that name before?

PETER: Jimmy Stewart.

HELEN: What d'you mean Jimmy Stewart! I'm talking about people we know, you dumdum, not some goddam film star! *(To BARBARA.)* Can you believe I'm married to a man like that? I mean – how stoopid can you get! *(Suddenly, to BARBARA.)* Hey – hey – don't you have a friend called Stewart? Weren't you talking about him the other day?

*BOB comes back to the sitting-room. Silence. BARBARA rises to her feet. She finds the courage to ask:*

BARBARA: Is everything all right?

BOB: Merry Christmas. He just rang up to say Merry Christmas.

*HELEN starts to sing, then JULIE joins in:*

'We wish you a merry Christmas;
We wish you a merry Christmas;
We wish you a merry Christmas and a happy
    New Year!'

*Despite their various hidden anxieties, BOB, BARBARA and PETER also join in, until, eventually, everyone is singing.*

'Good tidings we bring to you and your
    kin;
We wish you a merry Christmas and a happy
    New Year!'

*Lights fade. The Christmas tree is removed.*

*HELEN steps forward to address the audience.*

HELEN: In nineteen fifty we had an apartment on East Seventy-First Street – nothing fancy, but I loved it. I've never been much of a home-maker, anyone'll tell you that, but that place was special, it was the kind of place I always wanted. The sun streamed in through the kitchen window. It was all yellow and bright and cheery and warm. I even made curtains for that window. One evening Peter came home early. 'The Rosenbergs have been arrested,' he said, 'We have to leave.' I looked at Peter. His mouth had gone dry. He moistened his lips with his tongue. 'When?' I asked. 'Now, right now, tonight. We got to get the hell out of here as fast as we can.' And that's what we did. We left our clothes in the closet, books on the shelves, food in the refrigerator. We could've stayed, I suppose, and taken our chances – but we didn't. And from then on, there was no looking back.

*HELEN exits. Lights up. Day.*

*BARBARA and BOB are in the kitchen; they stand facing STEWART who has entered.*

STEWART: Sorry to disturb your Saturday, but I thought you'd be glad to know that it'll soon be over.

BARBARA: Over...?

STEWART: As far as you're concerned, anyway.

BARBARA: *(Not a question.)* The girls will be going.

STEWART: They will indeed.

BOB: When?

STEWART: As from today.

*BARBARA and BOB stare at each other, amazed.*

BARBARA: What's happened? I mean – why today? Has anything happened?

STEWART: Not yet. But with any luck...

*He allows the sentence to drift away into an infuriatingly ambiguous silence.*

BARBARA: *(Sharply.)* What? With any luck what?

*STEWART responds to the anger in her voice; his reply is unusually direct and unveiled.*

STEWART: Harry – the man from Portland, remember? – the man I told you about – well, he's on his way to London with his girlfriend. We believe that they will have another meeting with Lonsdale. If they do, we shall arrest them.

*Silence.*

BOB: What about Helen and Peter?

STEWART: Yes, we'll pick them up this afternoon. If everything goes according to plan. *(BARBARA sits suddenly, as if her legs can no longer support her.)* To tell you the truth, we're not entirely happy with this arrangement – we would have preferred to wait a little longer. But the Admiralty ran out of patience. My chief was overruled at Cabinet level – and there's no arguing with that.

*There is another moment of silence; both BARBARA and BOB are too stunned to speak. Eventually, BOB asks:*

BOB: Helen and Peter. What have they done?
How are they involved with this man Lonsdale?

STEWART: They're his transmitting station. Lonsdale brings them information they send back to KGB headquarters – either hidden in the books Mr Kroger posts to fictitious clients in various parts of Europe or by radio. I'm pretty sure we'll find a radio transmitter hidden somewhere in that house of theirs. I'm sorry to tell you so bluntly, but there's no doubt about it: your friends are both Communist agents with a good many years experience behind them. And their name's not Kroger, by he way. It's Cohen. Morris and Lona Cohen. They're American, not Canadian.

*Silence. BARBARA sits motionless.*

BARBARA: When I think of all the hours she's spent in this house. In this room. *(She lapses into silence for a moment; then she looks at STEWART.)* Was it all a lie – I mean – I can't believe that everything she told us – *(Almost imploringly.)* – was it?

STEWART: Well, not everything, I suppose.

BARBARA: I mean all those stories about her life on the farm with Aunt Sophie – was that the truth?

STEWART: Apparently not. Her parents emigrated from Poland. They lived in a place called Utica in New York State. Her father was fairly well-off; he made his money during Prohibition. He was a bootlegger. Peter Kroger used to be a school teacher. He became a Communist in the thirties and fought in the Spanish Civil War.

*Pause. BARBARA sits hunched on the sofa with her head bowed.*

BARBARA: How could she do it? How could she. *(Pause.)* I've never had many friends, not close friends, not people I felt really close to – never. But I trusted Helen. I thought she was brash and noisy and sometimes a bit silly. But I trusted her. I loved her.

STEWART: Well, I'm quite sure that her affection for you is perfectly genuine. There's no reason to doubt that.

BARBARA: *(Angry.)* No reason...? What do you mean, no reason? There's every reason to doubt everything she's ever said or done!

*(Silence.)* I wish you'd never come here, Mr Stewart.

STEWART: *(Gently.)* Yes, I'm sure...

BARBARA: I wish you'd never set foot inside this house!

BOB: Don't let's start blaming Mr Stewart – it's not his fault.

BARBARA: *(To STEWART, ignoring BOB.)* Helen may have lied to us – but you've gone one better. You made us do the lying; we've even lied to our own daughter.

BOB: We haven't lied to her.

BARBARA: We haven't told her the truth, have we? How do you think she's going to feel when she finds out?

BOB: She'll understand.

BARBARA: Will she?

BOB: Of course she will.

STEWART: I'm sure she'll realise you were only trying to protect her.

BARBARA: Oh, do stop making excuses. Helen's lying and we're lying – we're all playing the same rotten game.

STEWART: Well, hardly.

BARBARA: Of course we are. What's the difference between one lie and another? When I hear you making excuses for what we've done, I feel sick with fear – physically sick! People like you can find excuses for anything.

BOB: Look, there's no point in upsetting yourself –

BARBARA: I'm not upsetting myself! I'm trying to explain how I feel – and I'm trying to face up to the fact that I've betrayed Helen just as much as she betrayed me.

STEWART: Not true, that's just not true.

BARBARA: Isn't it?

BOB: *(Shouting.)* Of course not!

> *Silence.*

> *SALLY comes down the stairs. She is wearing outdoor clothes and carrying an unplugged phone. She taps on the kitchen door, opening it a fraction.*

SALLY: Excuse me, sir, I'm going now.

STEWART: Yes, all right.

> *With a brief embarrassed glance at the Jacksons, SALLY exits through the back door. STEWART turns to BOB.*

STEWART: I'll come back tomorrow, when everything's over and done with.

> *STEWART goes to the door.*

BARBARA: What'll happen to them?

> *STEWART pauses; he looks back at BARBARA.*

STEWART: The Krogers? They'll be sent for trial, I suppose. And then imprisoned.

BARBARA: But they love each other. They're happy together – and now they'll be separated. Perhaps for ever.

> *STEWART hesitates for a moment before he replies.*

STEWART: I'm sorry I've caused you so much pain. I only wish there was something I could do. I keep saying the same old thing, don't I? But there's nothing else I can say; nothing I can do; nothing any of us can do.

BARBARA: You could have told us the truth. You knew all this ages ago. Why didn't you tell us?

*STEWART hesitates before he replies.*

STEWART: I had to be careful. You might've warned the Krogers.

BARBARA: What makes you think I won't now?

STEWART: *(Attempting a confident smile.)* Well...

BARBARA: If I was brave enough, I would. I would. Really I would. *(Her eyes fill with tears.)* If I was brave enough, I'd go across the road – I'd bang on their door, and I'd say to them, 'Get out – get out before they catch you – please, please, get out – please...!'

*The front door bell rings. Everyone freezes. BARBARA goes to the sitting-room window and looks out.*

BARBARA: It's Helen!

*They all converse in hushed, urgent whispers.*

BOB: It can't be!

BARBARA: Well, it is.

*The doorbell rings again.*

STEWART: Answer the door, Mr Jackson.

BARBARA: Don't let her in – for God's sake don't let her in!

STEWART: Answer the door! She knows you're here.

BARBARA: Oh God...!

*BARBARA flees back to the kitchen. BOB goes to the hall. STEWART follows BARBARA. BOB opens the front door. HELEN enters.*

HELEN: Hi, Bob – how's life?

BOB: Oh well, you know. Not so bad.

HELEN: Is Barbara home?

BOB: Well, yes – but she's feeling a bit off-colour.

HELEN: Off-colour...?

BOB: Tired, you know.

HELEN: Why didn't you call me? I'd have come over and cooked lunch. *(She goes to the sitting-room.)* Where is she? Barbara!

*STEWART gestures to BARBARA, urging her to go to the sitting-room.*

BOB: She's not ill – just tired.

HELEN: It's not good, being tired all the time.

BOB: Just one of those things.

*BARBARA goes to the sitting-room. STEWART remains in the kitchen, a motionless silent shape in the shadows.*

HELEN: Barbara, honey – what is it? What's the matter?

BARBARA: It's nothing – really.

BOB: She's got a rotten headache.

HELEN: Again? You ought to see a doctor, sweetheart.

BARBARA: Yes, well...

HELEN: You make her go, Bob – she won't go unless you make her.

BOB: Yes, I will.

HELEN: Gee, you're looking real pale. Are you sure it's just a headache?

BARBARA: Quite sure.

HELEN: There's a lot of flu about. Maybe it's flu.

BARBARA: It's just another silly headache.

HELEN: Headaches aren't silly. Are you sure there's nothing wrong?

BARBARA: *(A little too sharply.)* Wrong?

BOB: *(Hastily.)* No, no, she's all right.

HELEN: It's not like you, getting all these headaches. You've had three in a month.

BARBARA: I suppose I'm a bit worried, that's all.

HELEN: What about?

BARBARA: Oh – this and that – things, you know.

HELEN: Things – what things?

BARBARA: Nothing special, nothing in particular, nothing serious.

HELEN: Come on – don't be shy. You just tell your Auntie Helen all about it.

BARBARA: It's nothing.

HELEN: Is it girl trouble? Make yourself scarce, Bob – let me talk to her alone.

BARBARA: No, it's nothing like that.

BOB: It's Julie and her exams.

BARBARA: *(Gratefully following BOB's lead.)* Yes, it's Julie and her exams.

HELEN: Don't worry about Julie – she'll be okay.

BOB: They're very important, these exams.

HELEN: She'll be okay, you know she will, she'll do fine.

BARBARA: Well, I hope so.

HELEN: You just stop worrying, sweetheart – otherwise you'll make yourself really ill.

BARBARA: Yes.

HELEN: I mean it.

BARBARA: Yes.

HELEN: So stop worrying, okay?

BARBARA: I'll try.

HELEN: That's my girl! *(Turning to leave.)* Where's Julie? Out with the boys?

BOB: She's gone to a hockey match.

HELEN: Give her my love. *(Going to the door.)* If I were you, honey, I'd go upstairs and have a proper rest.

*Deciding that it is now safe to go to leave, STEWART makes a move towards the kitchen door.*

BARBARA: Yes, all right.

HELEN: Go to bed and pamper yourself. Bob'll bring you a cup of tea, won't you, Bob?

BOB: Of course.

HELEN: Make a fuss of yourself. You deserve it. *(She pauses by the door.)* Hey, listen – before I go – there's something I ought to tell you.

*STEWART freezes at the back door.*

BARBARA: What's that?

HELEN: Peter and I have been – well, we've been thinking about the future.

BOB: What about it?

HELEN: I've been kinda low just recently – the January blues, I guess. Anyway, we both think it's time to move on.

BARBARA: } Move on...?

　　　　　} *(Together.)*

BOB: 　　} Move where?

HELEN: Peter's got some friends in Australia. We're thinking of packing our bags and going over there for six months or so. It's only an idea, of course, but Peter seems pretty keen.

*BARBARA and BOB exchange a brief glance.*

BOB: Well, that's – that's quite a big idea.

HELEN: Sure is. *(She grins.)* Just think of it: all that sun – Bondi beach – all those sexy young Aussies just waiting for Helen Kroger to put in an appearance. Sounds good, eh? Just poifeck.

BOB: Yes, it sounds marvellous.

BARBARA: Yes, it does – it's a marvellous idea, Helen.

HELEN: You think so?

BARBARA: Yes, I do – I think you should go away.

*HELEN smiles.*

HELEN: Trying to get rid of us, huh?

BARBARA: No, seriously – I think you should – it'd do you good, a change of scene – I really think you should go, Helen.

HELEN: Well, maybe.

BARBARA: *(Urgently.)* No really – I mean it – don't waste time – if you feel like going, go now!

*HELEN stares at BARBARA. The phone rings. Because she is standing beside HELEN at the sitting-room door, BARBARA has no choice but to answer the call.*

BARBARA: *(Despairingly.)* God – oh God!

*BARBARA goes to the phone. BOB rightly suspects that HELEN is puzzled by BARBARA's uncharacteristically emotional behaviour; he tries to ease the atmosphere with a light-hearted explanation.*

BOB: The phone never stops these days – and it's always for Julie.

BARBARA: *(On the telephone.)* Hello? – oh, hello, Maureen –

BOB: *(Grinning at HELEN.)* See what I mean?

*STEWART makes his escape.*

BARBARA: *(On the telephone.)* What? – No, she's not; she's gone down to the Sports Centre… When, this evening?... Yes, all right – Yes – Yes, I'll tell her – hang on a minute – *(Writing*

*a note.)* – Fourteen Hillcroft Road – Yes, I'll tell her – 'Bye-
'bye, Maureen, 'bye-'bye.

*BARBARA hangs up. She and HELEN stand facing each other.
HELEN's expression is grave and concerned.*

HELEN: Are you sure there's nothing wrong?

BARBARA: Quite sure.

HELEN: Well, you just let me know if there's anything I can
do, okay?

BARBARA: Okay.

HELEN: Take care of her, Bob – she's a very special lady.
Ciao!

*BOB lets her out of the front door. BARBARA goes to the hall.*

BARBARA: I think I'll go and lie down.

BOB: Would you like a cup of tea?

BARBARA: That'd be lovely.

*She walks up the stairs. BOB watches her go, then goes to the kitchen.
He fills the electric kettle at the sink, plugs it in, and stands waiting
for it to boil.*

*Slow fade to black. (BOB goes into the garden, leaving the back
door open.) Distant church bells, followed by 'Family Favourites'
on the radio.*

*Lights up. BOB and STEWART can be heard approaching from the
garden.*

STEWART: Is Julie not here?

BOB: She's gone down to the shops. After you, sir. *(They enter
the kitchen.)* They forgot to send the Sunday paper.

*BOB turns off the radio.*

STEWART: Ah. *(Beat.)* So she doesn't know? She didn't see
anything?

BOB: No.

STEWART: No – well, there wasn't much to see.

*BARBARA comes down the stairs.*

BARBARA: Good morning, Mr Stewart.

STEWART: Good morning, Mrs Jackson.

BARBARA: Let's go to the sitting-room.

*They go to the sitting-room. BARBARA switches on the electric fire. A brief, rather uneasy, silence.*

BOB: Everything went off all right, then?

STEWART: Oh, yes. Absolutely according to plan.

BOB: What, um – *(He hesitates, perhaps afraid to learn the truth.)* – what actually happened?

STEWART: We picked up Lonsdale and his two chums outside the Old Vic, then we came here. It was about half-past six – perhaps you saw the car?

BOB: We weren't looking.

STEWART: No, well – Superintendent Smith told the Krogers that they were going to be arrested on suspicion of offences against the Official Secrets Act. Mrs Kroger asked if she could go and stoke the boiler before they left the house, but Smith was naturally suspicious. He had a look in her handbag. He found a six-page letter in Russian, apparently from Lonsdale to his wife, a glass slide containing three microdots and a typed sheet of numbers, presumably some sort of a code. *(A small smile.)* I'm not surprised she wanted to stoke the boiler. *(Brief pause.)* I was right about the radio transmitter. It was hidden under the kitchen floor.

*Silence.*

BARBARA: Where are they now?

STEWART: Bow Street Police Station. *(Beat.)* I'm afraid you'll have the Press poking around for a week or so – it's a damn good story, you can't blame them. But after that, all being well, you'll be left in peace. *(Another smile.)* Normal service will be resumed as soon as possible, as they say on the television.

BOB: Will we have to go to court?

STEWART: Oh no, there'll be no need for that. We'll make sure that your names aren't even mentioned.

*The front door opens and JULIE enters; she is carrying a Sunday newspaper.*

JULIE: Mum, what's going on?

BOB: In here, Julie.

*JULIE enters the sitting-room.*

JULIE: Oh hello, Mr Stewart.

STEWART: Hello, Miss Jackson.

JULIE: There's a whole crowd of people in Auntie Helen's house – what's going on?

BARBARA: Oh Julie...

STEWART: Yes, perhaps I should explain –

JULIE: *(Suddenly alarmed.)* Has something happened?

STEWART: Yes, I'm afraid so – in fact – well, the truth is, they've been arrested.

JULIE: Arrested...?!

BARBARA: We couldn't tell you, Julie...

BOB: *(Overlapping.)* It was for your own good.

BARBARA: *(Overlapping.)* We couldn't tell you it was them.

JULIE: But why – what's happened?

STEWART: They're the ones we've been watching.

JULIE: Auntie Helen and Uncle Peter...?

STEWART: We had to find out, you see, we had to be sure – that's why we came here.

JULIE: Find out what?

STEWART: Evidence. We had to have proof that they were passing on secrets.

JULIE: What do you mean?

STEWART: They're spies. They're working for the Russians.

*Silence.*

JULIE: *(Barely audible.)* I don't believe it.

BARBARA: It's true darling, really it is. *(JULIE gasps; her hands fly to her face; BARBARA goes to her.)* Oh Julie, my Julie, I'm so sorry.

JULIE: *(Louder.)* I don't believe it.

BOB: Mum's right, it's true.

*BARBARA embraces JULIE; they are both weeping.*

BARBARA: We wanted to tell you but we couldn't, we didn't know what to do.

JULIE: How could she do it? How could she do it? How could she do it?

BARBARA: Oh Julie don't – please don't – please!

JULIE: *(Her voice rising.)* No – I don't believe it – no – I don't believe it – no!

*JULIE breaks away from BARBARA and runs upstairs.*

BARBARA: *(A terrible cry of anguish.)* Julie!

*Lights close on BOB as he steps forward to address the audience.*

BOB: Julie went up to her room. She gathered together all the things that Helen and Peter had ever given her – the handkerchiefs, the necklace, the silk blouse: she took them out into the garden and burnt them. *(Beat.)* A few days later, Mr Stewart came to the house with a present for Barbara: a thank-you present, he said, for looking after his girls for all those weeks. A box of six fish knives and forks. Silver plated. *(Beat.)* The Krogers were sentenced to twenty years imprisonment. Helen was a colonel in the KGB. She outranked Peter. After eight years in prison they were exchanged for an Englishman who had been jailed by the Russians. Julie's bitterness did not last. Curious to see her Auntie Helen again, she went to visit her in Holloway Prison. Towards the end of their conversation, Helen said: 'I'll never forgive your mother – never.' *(Beat.)* In 1969, when they were released from prison, the Krogers flew to Poland to start a new life. A crowd of journalists watched them go. 'Let's all be friends', said Helen. *(Beat.)* A few weeks later – a Sunday afternoon, it was – Barbara went into the kitchen, sat down on a chair, and died. A heart attack. She was so young, still in her fifties. *(Beat.)* I miss her more as time goes by. More not less. Is it always like that?

*Lights fade.*

*End.*

Printed in the USA
CPSIA information can be obtained
at www.ICGtesting.com
LVHW012009041124
795688LV00046B/1487